Take a PaDDLe

Western New York

Quiet Water for Canoes & Kayaks

Rich & Sue Freeman

Burford Books

Printed in the United States of America.

10 9 8 7 6 5 4 3 2 1

ISBN: 978-158080-185-0

Library of Congress Cataloging-in-Publication Data is on file with the Library of Congress.

Cover Design by Lynch Graphics and Design (www.bookcoverdesign.com)

Maps by Rich Freeman
Pictures by Rich & Sue Freeman
Author photo by Andrew Olenick (www.fotowerks.com)

Authors' Note

Every effort has been made to provide accurate and up-to-date waterway descriptions in this book. Hazards are noted where known, but conditions change constantly. Users of this book are reminded that they alone are responsible for their own safety when on any waterway and that they paddle the routes described in this book at their own risk.

The authors, publishers, and distributors of this book assume no responsibility for any injury, misadventure, fines, arrests or loss occurring from use of the information contained herein.

If you find inaccurate information or substantially different conditions (after all, things do change), please send a note detailing your findings to:

Burford Books, 101 E State St., Ithaca, NY 14850
or e-mail: info@burfordbooks.com

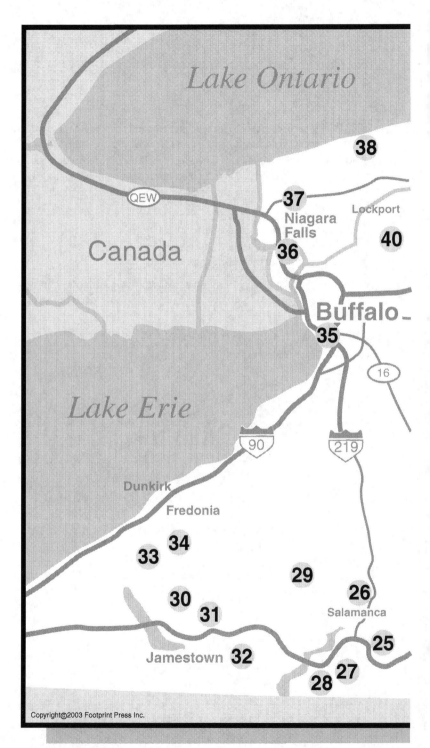

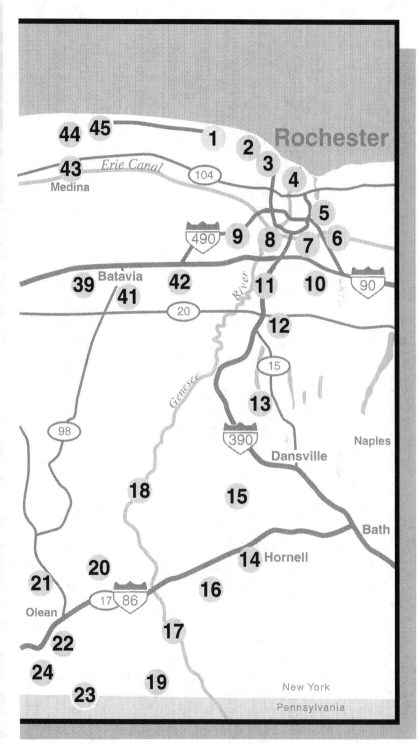

44 45
1 2 3 Rochester
43 *Erie Canal* 104 4
Medina
5
490 9 8 7 6
Batavia 42 River 11 10 90
39 41
20 12
15
13
98 390
Dansville Naples
18 15
Bath
14 Hornell
20
21 16
17 86
Olean 17
22
24 19
23 New York
Pennsylvania

Contents

Acknowledgments

The research, writing, production, and promotion of a book such as this is never a solitary adventure. *Take A Paddle - Western New York Quiet Water for Canoes & Kayaks* came into being because of the assistance of many wonderful people who freely shared their knowledge, experience, resources, thoughts, and time. We extend our heartfelt thanks to them all. Each in his or her own way is responsible for making Western New York a better place to live and, most of all, a region rich with the spirit of collaboration for the betterment of all. This is what ensures quality of life.

We particularly want to thank the people who volunteered as field editors. For our previous 8 guidebooks we personally hiked, biked and explored every trail and waterway listed. But, for this book, paddling every waterway posed a monumental task, requiring an enormous amount of time. If we paddled every waterway, the book would have been obsolete before we completed the research. To speed up the process, we enlisted the help of other paddlers to act a field editors. They paddled some of the waterways and reported back to us with data for this book. Or, they took along our draft data and maps and critiqued them as they paddled. This allowed us to offer a more comprehensive guidebook and do it in a timely manner. Our thanks goes to Laura Arney, Andy Hill and Ray & Carolyn Shea.

Thanks also to Susan Domina, our friend and able proofreader. Because of her attention to detail and grammatical expertise, this book is more consistent, more complete and sports fewer typographical errors. We'd like to believe it's error free but that proves to be an elusive goal that we've yet to achieve in our guidebooks.

Finally, our heartfelt thanks to Andy Olenick, a professional photographer, owner of Fotowerks, Ltd. and a personal friend of ours. He took time from his busy work schedule to capture us on film in outdoor settings. We appreciate his professionalism, his generosity, and his friendship.

Introduction

Paddle sports are growing in popularity. Chances are if you've picked up this guide you're already familiar with the joys of paddling. You can paddle rapidly to get an aerobic workout or go slowly and quietly to enjoy an up-close view of wildlife afforded by few other modes of transportation.

This is not a how-to-paddle guide. Many books and instructors are available to teach you how to paddle or to fine tune your skills. See the index at the back for some local options.

A group learning the basics of kayaking on
a Pack, Paddle, Ski adventure trip.

This guide will show you where to go and allow you to choose locations based on your skill level, time availability, and many other factors. It will probably also lead you to locations that you never knew existed as paddling options. That's a good thing. We don't have to travel around the world to find new adventures. They're often available close to home, if we only know where to look.

The waterways included are meant for beginning to intermediate paddlers or for those who enjoy the serenity of flat-water. We left out white water streams although in spring conditions some otherwise mild-mannered streams can offer white water. That's why we also recommended the best season for paddling each waterway.

Our goal is to get more people outdoors to enjoy the wonders of Western New York and to get current paddlers out more often. Have fun exploring the region by canoe or kayak.

If you enjoy this book please help spread the word by posting a review to your favorite online bookstore.

Rights of Passage

The courts of New York State consider rivers and streams as "public highways" if they are navigable. This dates back to English common law that prevailed when our country was founded, when waterways were the major routes of travel.

Everyone has the right to paddle a navigable river or stream even if the shores are privately owned. We do not, however, have the right to picnic or camp on private property, nor to cross privately-owned property to reach the water. You can legally get out of a boat to walk the waterway or shore (to the minimum extent necessary) to scout rapids or portage around an obstacle.

Generally the state, county or city owns the land near bridges and the roads that run next to water, so access is usually permitted in these areas. Public parks, DEC fishing access sites and state and locally owned launch sites are also available. Please obey all posted signs that you encounter.

Dogs Welcome

Many dog owners enjoy taking their companions along when exploring the outdoors - even paddling in a canoe. You must be able to control your dog to make sure an outdoor adventure is enjoyable to everyone around you, including the wildlife. Dogs are required to be leashed at a few public launches. Most waterway access points have no dog restrictions.

There are many waterways listed in this book that welcome dogs. Please respect the requirement that dogs be leashed where noted.

Safety Tips & Precautions

Paddling is a sport that can be enjoyed from spring through fall by people of wildly differing abilities, ages, and expertise. To stay safe, everyone must follow simple rules of common sense and caution which include:

- Know how to swim before setting foot in a canoe or kayak.
- Always wear a personal flotation device when in a canoe or kayak. (New York State law requires that you have access to a PFD, a personal flotation device.)
- Wear footwear to avoid sharp objects and poison ivy.
- Keep a good distance from dams - both from above and below. You could get pulled into a sluiceway, get caught in fast currents or eddies, or otherwise loose control of your boat.
- Respect the rights of property owners and obey all posted signs.
- Fast moving water can be dangerous and deadly. Use judgement in choosing to paddle a fast moving stream based on your experience and skill level. A swift current can tip your boat and pin you below water level at a strainer. You'd be amazed at how quickly it can happen. (Note the voice of personal experience here.) Never paddle during spring flood conditions.
- Cold water can be dangerous and deadly. Be especially careful if you go paddling early in the spring. It is tempting to go paddling on early warm days. Remember the water is still cold. If you do not have specialized clothing, try a few of these ideas. Keep your hands warm with rubber dishwashing gloves. If you want to keep your feet warm, try knee high rubber boots instead of neoprene booties or water shoes. If you are not dressed to swim in a lake, paddle near shore so you can get to shore quickly in the event of a capsize. Paddle where wind is not as likely to be a factor, like early in the day or on smaller bodies of water. Be sure to wear your PFD as you will not be able to swim long in cold water if you swamp. Modern PFDs are comfortable and can help keep you warm. Often the air is colder on the water than on the land. Wear a hat to conserve body heat. Take extra clothes with you and put them in your boat

wrapped in 2 or 3 plastic bags and seal them. Wear synthetic clothes, not cotton.

• Always take emergency supplies with you, in a waterproof bag, tied securely in your boat. These should include water, snacks, flashlight, sun lotion, emergency space blanket, compass, knife, waterproof matches and a first aid kit.

• Let someone know where you're going and when you expect to return. As a minimum, leave a note that someone looking for you could find.

While doing research for this guidebook, we paddled many miles of gorgeous ponds, creeks and rivers. We experienced wildlife up close, watched the mist dissipate from streams in early morning and thrilled to new discoveries around each bend. We also had some hair-raising experiences. The waterways where these occurred are not detailed in this book, but we do mention them so you know why we left the sections out. For instance, Tonawanda Creek from Attica to Batavia was a harrowing 5 miles of constant logjams in deep mud banks that left Rich utterly exhausted. Sue's turn at exhaustion came with a segment through Bergen Swamp on Black Creek which was also blocked with a seemingly endless series of log-jams. Instead of dealing with portages over high mud banks, Sue had to put up with knee deep nettles that sent razor sharp barbs into her legs and rampant poison ivy that left reminders long after the portaging was done.

These segments aren't in this book. Still, river and creek conditions can change rapidly with rising waters and falling trees. So a segment that we found easy and clear on our first visit can pose a problem in future years. It is impossible to predict obstructions in any given section, as one storm could change safety significantly. Paddle with caution and at your own risk.

Legend

At the beginning of each waterway listing, you will find a description with some or all of the following information:

Location: The towns and counties where the waterway is located or through which it passes.

Directions: How to find the launch point parking area from a major road or town.

Many DEC launch sites are labeled with brown and yellow signs like this one for Guilford Lake.

Launch Site: More detailed information about a launch site. There may be multiple launch sites listed that give you the option of shortening your trip.

Take-out Site: More detailed information about a take-out site. There may be multiple take-out sites listed that give you the option of shortening your trip.

Best Season to Visit: The season when you're more likely to find favorable padding conditions. However, water levels are affected by many factors so there is never a definitively perfect time to paddle.

Nearby Campgrounds: Contact information for any campgrounds that are on or near the waterway.

Paddling Distance: The paddling distance in miles for the segment described in the paddling directions. Distance segments are also listed if there are multiple launch and take-out options.

Estimated Time to Paddle: A rough approximation of how much time it will take to paddle this route. However, time can be affected by many factors such as type of craft paddled, strength and skill of the paddlers, rate of water flow, depth of water over rocks, wind conditions, frequency of impediments encountered that require portaging, number and duration of rest breaks taken, etc.

Difficulty: A rating of the level of difficulty of the paddling experience. All waterways listed in this guide are class I water.

1 Paddle – Very Easy – A flat water pond or a wide waterway with negligible current. Suitable for beginners or a leisurely paddle by anyone.

2 Paddles – Easy – A slowly moving waterway with low probability of encountering impediments. Suitable for beginners.

3 Paddles – Moderate – A waterway with moving current and manageable obstacles such as riffles and downed trees. Suitable for intermediate paddlers.

4 Paddles – Strenuous – A waterway with swift current and obstacles such as riffles and downed trees. Suitable for advanced intermediate paddlers.

Water Level Information: A web site or phone number where information can be obtained on current and/or historical water levels for this waterway. Use this information to judge if the water is too shallow or conversely, too deep (flooded) or moving too fast for safe paddling.

Other Activities: A description of what you can do on or near this waterway besides paddle.

Amenities: Services and resources you'll find along this waterway.

Dogs: Tells if dogs are or are not allowed, or if they're required to be on a leash.

Admission: The entrance fee, if there is one, to use the area.

Contact: The address and phone number of the organization to contact if you would like additional information or if you have questions not answered in this book.

Maps

This book is loaded with sketch maps to give you an idea of where to find each waterway and how to navigate once you get there. We've found the *New York State Atlas & Gazetteer* by DeLorme to be a valuable asset when trying to find a launch site in unknown territory. And of course the many mapping resources available on the internet can be helpful as well.

Water access directions are listed as upstream, left or right and downstream, left or right. They are defined from the paddler's perspective as he or she is paddling downstream as per the diagram below:

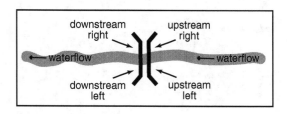

Map Legend

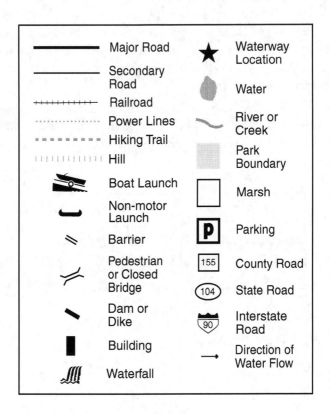

———————	Major Road	★	Waterway Location
———————	Secondary Road		Water
+++++++++++	Railroad		
············	Power Lines		River or Creek
■ ■ ■ ■ ■	Hiking Trail		Park Boundary
┆┆┆┆┆┆┆┆	Hill		
	Boat Launch		Marsh
	Non-motor Launch	**P**	Parking
≶	Barrier	155	County Road
✕	Pedestrian or Closed Bridge	(104)	State Road
╲	Dam or Dike	90	Interstate Road
■	Building	→	Direction of Water Flow
∭	Waterfall		

Paddles in Monroe, Livingston and Steuben Counties

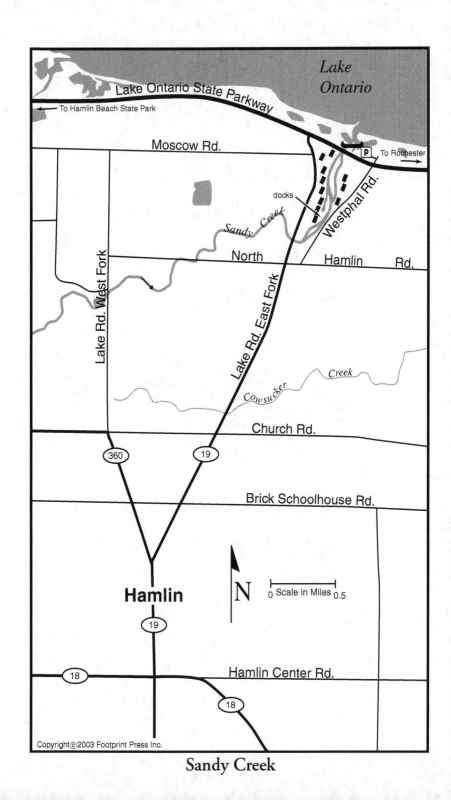

Sandy Creek

1

SANDY CREEK

Location: Hamlin, Monroe County

Directions: From Lake Ontario State Parkway (east of Hamlin Beach State Park) turn north onto Westphal Road. The large parking area and boat launch sits at the corner of Westphal and Lake Ontario State Parkway.

Launch and Take-out Site: Drive to the launch to unload your boat then return your vehicle 0.1 mile to the parking area. The launch has a paved ramp and docks, downstream, right of the bridge.

Best Season to Visit: Early spring when water is high or fall when there's less boat traffic

Paddling Distance: 3 to 4 miles round trip

Estimated Time to Paddle: 2 hours round trip

Difficulty: ▬◖

Other Activities: Fish

Amenities: Porta-potties near parking lot off Westphal Road.

Dogs: OK

Admission: Free

Field Contributors: Ray and Carolyn Shea

Sandy Creek is one of those common names like Buttermilk Falls and Main Street. There are several Sandy Creeks in New York State. This one is 15 miles west of Rochester and flows north into Lake Ontario. Several marinas cluster near its outlet and provide motorboat access to Lake Ontario. However, paddle upstream against a very slow current, and you'll leave most of the motorboats and cottages behind. Depending on water level, 1.5 to 2 miles upstream the waterway will become too rocky and shallow even for a canoe or kayak. At this point, head back downstream. This is a short, easy paddle with an easy-to-find launch but lacks the abundant wildlife of more remote areas.

Paddling Directions:

- Head south, upstream, under the brown Lake Ontario State Parkway bridge that sits on red medina sandstone pillars. Pass two small marinas and several cottages.
- Once past the quaint little marina called Sleepy Hollow, you can paddle on either side of small islands.
- Pass under the Route 19 bridge on cement pillars.
- Pass under the green metal North Hamlin Road bridge.
- At 1.5 to 2 miles, depending on water level, it will get too shallow to proceed. Turn around and paddle downstream.
- Pass the launch and continue under the Lake Ontario State Parkway bridge to explore the small bays and marshland before the Lake Ontario shore.

Date visited:

Notes:

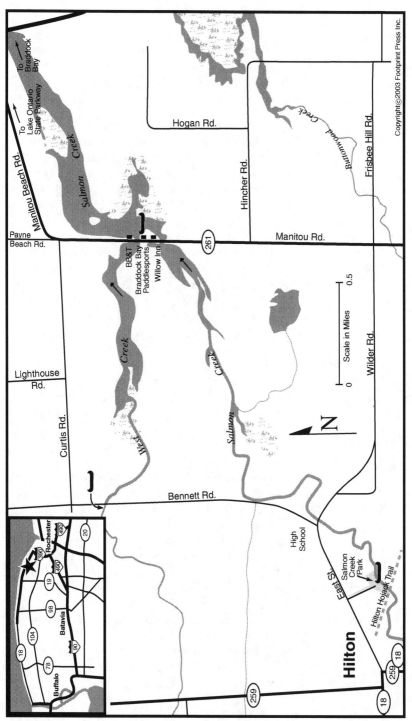

Salmon and West Creeks

2

SALMON & WEST CREEKS

Location: Hilton and Parma, Monroe County

Directions: From Lake Ontario State Parkway, exit at Manitou Beach Road (Route 261) and head south to Braddock Bait & Tackle, Docksiders or Willow Inn. Or, from Route 104, turn north on Manitou Road (Route 261) to Willow Inn, Docksiders or Braddock Bait & Tackle.

Launch Site #1: Braddock Bay Paddlesports, 416 Manitou Road, Hilton, (585) 392-2628, www.paddlingny.com, $3 for nice carpeted wood sloped launch.

Willow Inn (an Irish Pub), 438 Manitou Road, Hilton, (585) 392-3489, charge $5 to launch and $3 to park, hand launch from a lumpy slab of cement.

Braddock Bait & Tackle, 372 Manitou Road, Hilton, (585) 392-6600, charge $5, cement boat ramp surrounded by mooring docks.

Launch Site #2: Salmon Creek Park off East Street in Hilton (Hilton Health Care Family Medicine is on the corner). Carry 25-yards across mowed grass to a cement platform in the creek or to a set of cement stairs a bit downstream. The ice storm of 2003 brought down several trees, so launching here requires portaging around downed trees.

Launch Site #3: Park along Bennett Road at the West Creek crossing and launch upstream, left via a grass slope. The ice storm of 2003 brought down several trees, so launching here requires portaging around downed trees.

Best Season to Visit: Spring for paddling downstream; any season for a round-trip from Route 261

Paddling Distance: West Creek between Route 261 and Bennett Road is 1.5 miles each way

Salmon Creek between Route 261 and Salmon Creek Park is 2.2 miles each way

Estimated Time to Paddle: 1-2 hours for each creek

Difficulty: ▸━▬ (round trip from Route 261)

▸━▬ ▸━▬ (launching from Bennett Road or Salmon Creek Park)

Other Activities: Fish, bird watch, dine or visit a bar

Amenities: Salmon Creek Park has a picnic pavilion and grills. Braddock Bait & Tackle sells snacks and drinks and has a canoe for rent. In front of BB&T is Braddock Bay Restaurant serving Italian American food. Docksiders and Willow Inn are bars.

Dogs: OK

Admission: Varies by location, see details under Launch Sites.

Leave busy Braddock Bay to the power boats and instead, venture upstream on West Creek through cattail marshes and water lilies. This area is a prime migration route for hawks and owls. Paddle here in mid- to late-April to catch the peak migration. Return in summer and fall for the profusion of white water lilies.

Salmon Creek has deeper water and is less likely to be choked with aquatic vegetation by late summer. There are plenty of side channels to explore. You can paddle to the East Street bridge (1.6 miles) before meeting downed trees and shallow-water riffles that block your way.

In spring you can put-in at Salmon Creek Park and paddle downstream on Salmon Creek or put-in from the Bennett Road bridge to paddle downstream on West Creek. Your challenge will be trees across the streams compliments of the 2003 ice storm.

Directions Round-trip from Route 261 (~2 hours):

- From any of the three launch spots on Route 261, paddle among the docks and motorboats.
- A low cement bridge marks the channel to West Creek. To save your ears, try to time your passage under the bridge between cars.
- The entrance to Salmon Creek is farther south, under a low green metal bridge.
- Paddle up the waterways and explore the side channels at will.
- Turn around when the water gets too shallow and paddle back to the launch.

Salmon Creek Paddling Directions (~1.5 hours):
- Launch at Salmon Creek Park and head downstream. It won't be long before you have to portage around downed trees.
- Paddle under the cement bridge with green rails at East Street.
- After sharp bends the creek will come close to Bennett Road then the waterway will get deeper and wider. It's 1.6 mile further to Route 261.
- Leave woods behind and continue through the cattail marsh. Explore side bays.
- Paddle under the green Route 261 bridge then turn left to find any of the three possible take-out points.

West Creek Paddling Directions (~1 hour):
- Launch at Bennett Road and head downstream. It won't be long before you have to portage around downed trees.
- Leave woods behind and continue through the cattail marsh. Explore side bays.
- Paddle under the low cement Route 261 bridge then turn left to take-out at Braddock Bait & Tackle or right for the other two take-outs.

Date visited:

Notes:

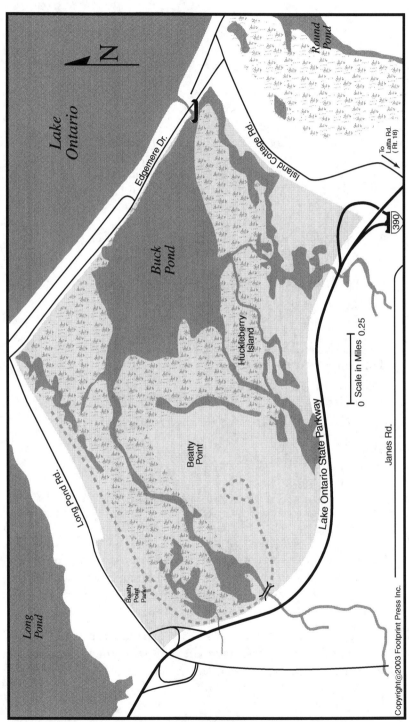

Buck Pond

3

BUCK POND

Location: Greece, Monroe County

Directions: From I-390 exit at Latta Road (Route 18) and turn right onto Latta Road. Take a quick left onto Island Cottage Road. Drive under the Lake Ontario State Parkway then turn left onto Edgemere Drive. A parking area will be on the left before the Buck Pond outlet.

Launch & Take-out Site: A 12-car parking area off Edgemere Drive offers a sloped gravel launch.

Best Season to Visit: Spring

Paddling Distance: The western channel from the launch to the trail bridge is 2.2 miles.

The eastern channel from the launch to the Lake Ontario State Parkway bridge is 1.1 miles.

Estimated Time to Paddle: 3 hours to explore both channels

Difficulty: ▶━━

Other Activities: Fish, bird watch

Amenities: A hiking trail (part of Beatty Point Park) crosses the red, cut-Medina sandstone bridge in the western channel.

Dogs: OK

Admission: Free

Contact: DEC, Region 8
6274 East Avon-Lima Road, Avon, NY 14414
(585) 226-2466

Unlike the other ponds that rim Lake Ontario north of Rochester, Buck Pond is not ringed with cottages. Your views will be of a cattail marsh. Civilization will infringe on your ears however, because you're never far from road noise on Lake Ontario State Parkway or motorboats on Lake Ontario and Long Pond.

In spring we found several sets of swans nesting here. On a calm day you can easily paddle across the open water to explore several meandering channels or even head out across the sand bar to paddle in Lake Ontario. By summer your views are impeded by high cattails and marsh vegetation and water lilies begin to choke the channels.

Paddling Directions:
- From the launch you can head left to explore the eastern channel or head across Buck Pond to explore the western channel or the channels around Huckleberry Island.

Date visited:

Notes:

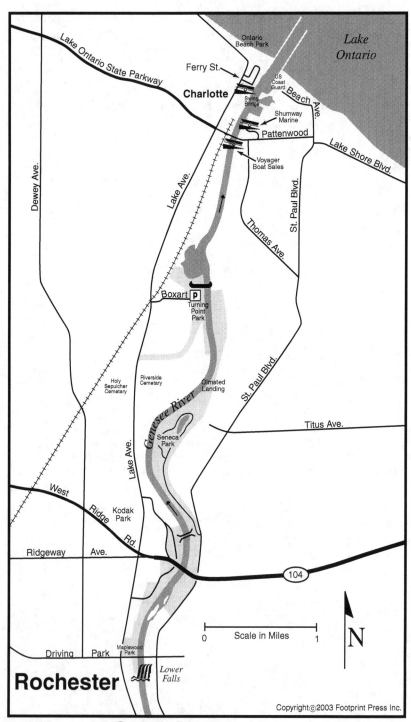

Genesee River (Charlotte Area)

4

GENESEE RIVER
(Charlotte Area)

Location:	Charlotte, Monroe County
Directions:	From Lake Avenue, turn east onto Boxart Street. Follow Boxart to the end where you'll find the Turning Point Park parking area. If the gate is open, you can drive to the left then downhill to the launch at water level. More likely, you'll have to carry your boat 0.3 mile down to the launch.
Launch Site #1:	Turning Point Park has a sloped launch. A wheeled cart is helpful for getting your boat to water level.
Launch Site #2:	Monroe County Boat Launch at Ontario Beach Park. From Lake Avenue turn east onto Ferry Street to the large parking area and paved boat launch which costs $6 Thursday through Sunday, Memorial Day through Labor Day. Otherwise, it's free.
Launch Site #3:	From Thomas Avenue turn west at the sign "Navy Point Yacht Sales and GYC" and drive under the O'Rorke bridge to Voyager Boat Sales. The cost is $4 to park and launch via the paved ramp.
Launch Site #4:	Shumway Marine off Pattenwood Drive has a commercial boat launch and offers free launching for canoes and kayaks.
Best Season to Visit:	Summer or fall
Paddling Distance:	Turning Point Park to Lower Falls: 3.8 miles Turning Point Park to Monroe County Boat Launch: 1.7 miles Monroe County Boat Launch to Lake Ontario: 0.9 mile
Estimated Time to Paddle:	3 hours upstream, round trip 1 to 2 hours downstream, round trip
Difficulty:	▬◖ ▬◖
Other Activities:	Fish, bird watch
Amenities:	Turning Point Park has hiking trails. Canoe rentals are offered evenings and weekends,

April through October. Call (585) 787-3370 for details.

Ontario Beach Park has a historic carousel, natural sand beach with guarded swimming, playground, picnic shelters, baseball diamond, bathhouse, beach volleyball courts, performance pavilion, food concessions, a boardwalk and a pier.

Dogs: OK
Admission: Free
Field Contributor: Laura Arney
Contact: City of Rochester Department of Parks
400 Dewey Avenue, Rochester, NY 14613
(585) 428-6770

Turning Point Park is a 112-acre wilderness setting in an urban environment. The term "Turning Point" has double meaning to the Charlotte residents nearby. Historically, the wide basin in the nearby Genesee River was a physical place that ships could turn around before encountering the Lower Falls. This was once a heavily used industrial area with ships visiting docks to load and unload coal, wheat, feldspar, paper boxes, and tourists. In 1913 over one million

The Veteran's Memorial Bridge (Route 104)
spans the Genesee River.

tons of coal was loaded onto lake ships here. It was an active port until the early 1970s. Car ferries operated round trips to Cobourg, Canada until 1942. Essroc Materials, Inc., Great Lakes Cement Division still operates on this site, and uses the docks at water level to unload dry cement to the large storage tanks which sit atop the cliff.

In 1972 the Rochester-Monroe County Port Authority announced plans to build an oil storage tank farm on the site. Area residents, led by Bill Davis, fought the plan, which would have bull-dozed a stand of 200-year-old oak trees and cut off community access to the river. They achieved a "turning point" in getting the city to turn away from commercial development of the river water-front and toward its recreational use. The city bought the land in 1976 and opened Turning Point Park in 1977.

History abounds along the area of the Genesee River gorge you'll paddle. The early settlements of McCrackenville, Carthage, King's Landing, Frankfort, and Castletown are all but memories. Only Charlotte remains a familiar name. With the coming of the Erie Canal, Rochesterville grew. By 1834 the combination of these seven settlements became the city of Rochester.

At this writing (2003) the Stutson Street bridge, which was built in 1917, was being replaced by the O'Rorke Bridge, which has a 2004 estimated completion date. The O'Rorke Bridge is a 994-foot long lift bridge. It's named after Colonel Patrick O'Rorke, a Rochester native and Civil War hero. To read his history, see web site: www.ororkebridge.com/Bio.htm.

By the time the Genesee River reaches this stretch it is a wide and powerful river. Don't attempt paddling here in spring. The water has traveled 158 miles from its source near Gold, Pennsylvania. You can paddle upstream (south) for 4 miles to below the 78-feet high Lower Falls or downstream (north) to Lake Ontario. Or, simply paddle around the cattail marshes near the turning basin area. You'll be deep inside the wooded Genesee River gorge. Upstream you're likely to pass many people fishing. Downstream you'll encounter motor and sailboat traffic that increases significantly as you near Lake Ontario.

Upstream (south) Paddling Directions:

- From Turning Point Park, head upstream past marshy shores.
- The marsh will give way to steep wooded shorelines.
- To the right will be a wooden dock at Olmsted Landing. Steep stairs up the gorge bank lead to Seneca Park.
- The Kodak King's Landing Water Treatment Plant will be to the right.
- Pass under the Monroe County Pure Water's Pedestrian Bridge which connects Seneca Park and Lake Avenue.
- Pass under the high arches of the Veteran's Memorial Bridge (Route 104).
- Pass the two Seth Green Islands. The current will increase.
- Lower Falls is shortly after the high arches of Driving Park Bridge. If the current is too strong, beach your boat and try walking the shore to get a bottom-up view of this impressive waterfall.
- Return downstream to Turning Point Park.

Downstream (north) Paddling Directions:

- From Turning Point Park, head downstream through the turning basin.
- Before long you'll be among a series of yacht clubs and marinas.
- Pass under the new O'Rorke Bridge, which is slated to be opened in 2004.
- Pass under the old Stutson Street bridge. This may eventually get torn down. (Voyager Boat Sales launch is to the right under this bridge.)
- The abandoned bridge in the middle of the channel is the Hojack Swing Bridge. It was built in 1905 by the long-defunct King Bridge Company to carry railroad traffic over the Genesee River. It sits on a central pivot point so it can swing open to allow boat traffic and close for train traffic. However, the rail line crossing the bridge was abandoned in the early 1990s, and the bridge sits unused. CSX Corp, who now owns the bridge, had been ordered by the U.S. Coast Guard to remove it, but that order was put on hold. Local historians want it to be deemed a landmark and saved, but

boaters and shippers who use the river want it destroyed. Visit www.savehojack.com to read about its history and the efforts to save it.

- The Monroe County Boat Launch will be on the left. Take out here or return upstream. Or, paddle through a long channel created by piers to reach Lake Ontario.

Date visited:

Notes:

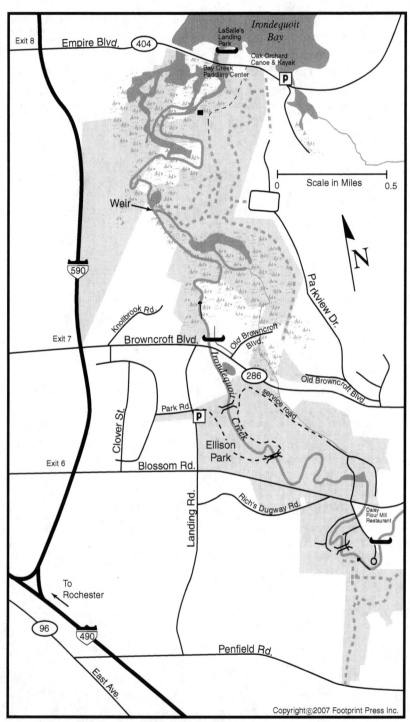

Irondequoit Creek (Ellison Park to Irondequoit Bay)

5

IRONDEQUOIT CREEK
(Ellison Park to Irondequoit Bay)

Location: Penfield and Irondequoit, Monroe County

Directions: From I-590 on the east side of Rochester, take exit 6 (Blossom Road) and head east on Blossom Road. Cross Landing Road, Tennis Court Drive, and Rich's Dugway Road, then take the next right. Bear left toward Circle Shelter, then cross over Irondequoit Creek. Parking for the canoe launch area is on the left near a small beige building.

Launch Site #1: The canoe launch in Ellison Park (near Circle Shelter) has a 12-car parking lot, picnic tables and a grill, and cement bank reinforcements that provide steps into the water.

Upstream Launch Site: Penfield has plans to build a launch site behind Panorama Plaza on Penfield Road. This will allow launching further upstream for a longer run.

Launch Site #2: From Browncroft Boulevard turn north onto Old Browncroft Boulevard, then immediately left. Park to the left of the Monroe County Pure Waters building. A 10-yard carry leads to a cement and wood deck launch area, downstream, right of the Browncroft Boulevard bridge.

Take-out Site: From I-590 on the east side of Rochester, take exit 8 (Empire Boulevard, Route 404) and head east on Route 404. When the road dips down to the base of Irondequoit Bay (the Dugway) turn left into LaSalle's Landing Park on the north (bay) side where Irondequoit Creek meets Irondequoit Bay. Walk northwest from the back of the parking area to find a sloped gravel hand launch. Development plans for this park call for addition of a pedestrian bridge and board-walk.

Best Season to Visit: Summer (water can be high and fast in spring and hunting is allowed along the shores in fall)

Paddling Distance: 4.5 miles

Ellison Park launch to Browncroft Blvd.: 2.2 miles

Browncroft Boulevard to the weir: 1.0 mile

The weir to LaSalle's Landing Park: 1.3 miles

Estimated Time to Paddle: 3 hours

Difficulty: (from Ellison Park)

(from Irondequoit Bay)

Water Level Information: http://waterdata.usgs.gov/ny/nwis/rt (the gage, #04232034, is significantly upstream of this segment, at Railroad Mills Road in Fishers)

Other Activities: Fish, bird watch, hike in Ellison Park

Amenities: Ellison Park has pavilions, picnic facilities, hiking trails, restrooms, tennis courts, and playgrounds.

Rental boats and shuttle service are available at Irondequoit Bay from Bay Creek Paddling Center, 1099 Empire Blvd., Rochester, NY 14609, (585) 288-2830, www.baycreek.com

Rental boats and shuttle service are available at Irondequoit Bay from Oak Orchard Canoe & Kayak, 1300 Empire Blvd., Rochester, NY 14609, (585) 288-5550 www.oakorchardcanoe.com

Dogs: OK on leash

Admission: Free

Contact: Monroe County Parks Department
171 Reservoir Avenue, Rochester, NY 14620
(585) 256-4950, www.monroecounty.gov

Field Contributor: Andy Hill

You have two options for paddling Irondequoit Creek. One is to start in Ellison Park (or upstream from behind Panorama Plaza in Penfield) and paddle downstream to Irondequoit Bay as described below. The second option is to start at Irondequoit Bay and paddle upstream a ways then turn around and return to the starting point. The current is not strong (except after significant spring melts or a heavy rain storm), so it's easy to do a round trip.

The cattail marshes between Browncroft and Empire Boulevards are fun to explore with lots of nooks and crannies. A variety of birds either live or migrate through here. Mute swans, green herons, moorhens, kingbirds and ducks have been spotted.

Irondequoit Creek north of the weir.

Depending on your luck and timing, you may encounter a clear channel and clean shores or significant blow downs and man-made garbage along the shores. Paddlers in 1996 reported garbage, but in 2003 we found an unpolluted and unimpeded route. You'll paddle through clear water in a sandy-bottomed creekbed lined in waving grasses. We thoroughly enjoyed paddling this waterway one summer day in the mid-1980s, in an inflatable canoe that leaked air and listed significantly to one side by the time we reached Irondequoit Bay.

Paddling Directions:
- From the canoe launch in Ellison Park, head right, downstream.
- Irondequoit Creek makes many sweeping curves on its journey through Ellison Park.
- Pass under a wooden pedestrian bridge.
- Pass under a wooden park road bridge.
- Watch for the historic Daisy Flour Mill (now a restaurant) to your right.

- Pass under a silver-railed bridge for Blossom Road.
- Pass two large culverts to your right.
- Pass under a cement and silver-railed park road bridge.
- Pass under 2 pedestrian bridges, then leave Ellison Park.
- At 2.2 miles, pass under the green highway bridge for Browncroft Boulevard (Route 286).
- To your right is a cement and wood deck launch site with access from the Monroe County Pure Waters road.
- The creek will enter a cattail marsh.
- At. 3.2 miles you'll pass a yellow caution sign, then a weir underwater that limits passage to boats with less than a 5 inch beam. It's generally easy to pass over this barrier, but can be challenging in low water conditions.
- Continue downstream to Irondequoit Bay on the main channel. (There are many side channels in the cattail marsh.)
- Pass Bay Creek Paddling Center on the right.
- Paddle under the green highway bridge of Empire Boulevard. Watch to the right for the end of a cement wall then a small gap in the cattails that marks the take-out: a sloped gravel hand launch into LaSalle's Landing Park.

    Note: You can continue out into Irondequoit Bay. If you turn right and follow the shore past Oak Orchard Canoe & Kayak, you'll find an area where the water rolls up to shore by wooden pillars. This makes a nice take-out point (assuming the winds are mild on Irondequoit Bay). Parking is available off Empire Boulevard.

Date visited:

Notes:

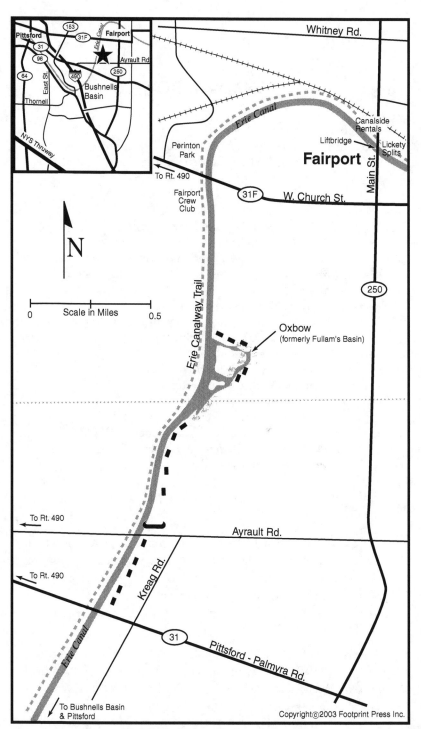

Erie Canal - Oxbow Loop

6

ERIE CANAL - OXBOW LOOP

Location: Perinton, Monroe County

Directions: From I-490 take exit 26 to Pittsford-Palmyra Road. Head east toward Palmyra and turn left at the first light onto Ayrault Road. Cross over the Erie Canal then turn left into the Town of Perinton Boat Launch.

Launch & Take-out Site: Town of Perinton Boat Launch on Ayrault Road has a 12-car parking lot, a Porta-potty, a paved boat ramp and 2 wooden docks.

Other Launch & Take-out Sites: See other points of interest below

Best Season to Visit: Spring, summer and fall

Paddling Distance: The Oxbow loop is 2.0 miles, round trip.
From the launch it's 2.5 miles downstream (to the right) to the liftbridge in Fairport.
From the launch it's 5.9 miles upstream (to the left) to Lock 32 in Pittsford.

Estimated Time to Paddle: 45 minutes round trip

Difficulty: ▶━━━ (negligible current)

Other Activities: Hike or bike the Erie Canalway Trail

Amenities: The Ayrault Road boat launch has a Porta-potty. Canalside Rentals rents boats, (585) 377-5980, www.canalsiderentals.com

Dogs: OK

Admission: Free

The coming of the Erie Canal brought settlement to this, once swampy area. The village of Perrin was named after its first settler, Glover Perrin. Slightly to the west, with a grocery store, a boat loading platform and post office, Fullam's Basin was named for Elisha Fullam. In 1829 the post office was moved from Fullam's Basin to Perrin. In 1853 Perrin was renamed the village of Fairport in the town of Perinton.

The original Erie Canal (Clinton's Ditch) had more curves than today's canal. When the canal was widened, deepened and rerouted south of Rochester, many loops and turns were eliminated. A straight embankment and towpath were built (today's Erie

Canalway Trail), allowing the water to fill the entire old loop creating a widewater. The widewater in Perinton (in what used to be Fullam's Basin) is called the Oxbow.

By the 1930s the Oxbow was dotted with summer cottages. These dilapidated into squatter homes by the 1970s, but only a few remain today. The islands in front of the Oxbow are the artificial result of many years of dredging. The northernmost channel is filling in with siltation and encroaching cattails, but it is still passable to paddle craft.

There have been four disasterous breaks in the canal in the Perinton area. The first occurred near Fullam's Basin a year after the canal was built. The second break was at the Oxbow in 1871 when a burrowing muskrat caused the collapse of a 510-foot section of the canal bank. The waters spilled out across the fields, carrying away barges and bridges. The third break was located at the embankment while the Barge Canal was being built. It caused heavy damage as thousands of tons of water poured out over the farmlands. The canal suffered its latest break in the 1970s, again at the Great Embankment in Bushnells Basin. It occurred when an engineering error resulted in the collapse of the canal into a storm sewer tunnel being constructed under the canal.

Paddling Directions - Oxbow Loop:
* From the launch, head downstream, right.
* Pass under overhead powerlines then turn right into the Oxbow channel.
* Pass a channel to the left.
* After some old cottages the channel ahead will dead-end. Turn left into the narrow, shallow channel through cattails.
* Turn left again when you reach a wider channel with new homes on the shore.
* At the main canal (marked by a group of wooden pilings), turn left and paddle back to the launch.

Other Points of Interest Downstream (from the Ayrault Road launch):
* 1.4 miles to the floating dock and boathouse (on the left) of the Fairport Crew Club (www.fairportcrew.org).
* 1.6 miles to the wooden docks of Perinton Park (left) with restrooms and canalside swings.
* 2.4 miles to the wooden docks (left) of Canalside Rentals.

Canoeing the Erie Canal near guard gates.

- 2.5 miles to the village of Fairport with Lickety Splits Ice Cream and Lift Bridge Cafe restaurant canalside (left, just past the liftbridge).

Other Points of Interest Upstream (from the Ayrault Road launch):
- 0.8 mile to the Bushnells Basin guard gates.
- 1.5 miles to Oliver Louds B&B and Richardson's Canal House restaurant (left) shortly before the Marsh Road bridge and Abbott's Ice Cream (left) shortly after the Marsh Road bridge.
- 2.7 miles to docks at Great Embankment Park (right).
- 3.2 miles to Cartersville guard gates.
- 4.3 miles to the village of Pittsford with shops and restaurants along Schoen Place.

Date visited:

Notes:

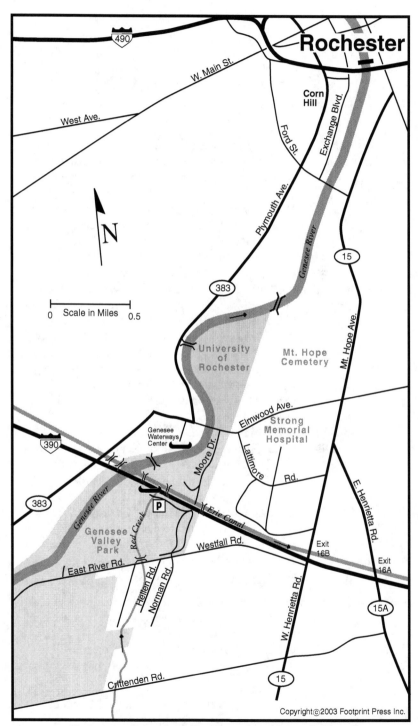

Genesee River, Erie Canal and Red Creek

GENESEE RIVER, ERIE CANAL & RED CREEK

Location: Rochester, Monroe County

Directions: From Elmwood Avenue, west of the Genesee River, turn into the parking area for the large building labeled "City of Rochester, Genesee Valley Arena." Drive through the parking area to the back lot at Genesee Waterways Center.

Launch & Take-out Site #1: Genesee Waterways Center off Elmwood Avenue has several segments of floating docks with easy, low water access.

Launch & Take-out Site #2: From Elmwood Avenue, east of the Genesee River, turn south onto Moore Drive into Genesee Valley Park. Continue over the canal then turn right. If the gate is closed, park on the left and carry to the launch. Otherwise continue straight, drive over Red Creek and park on the right, underneath the I-390 bridges. Big, flat rocks along shore make easy launching from either shore of Red Creek.

Best Season to Visit: Spring, summer and fall

Paddling Distance: The trip described (from Genesee Waterways Center, up the Genesee River, east on the canal and up Red Creek to Crittenden Road) is 3.6 miles round trip.
Genesee Waterways Center to Red Creek: 0.5 mile
Red Creek from canal to Crittenden: 1.3 miles
Genesee Waterways Ctr. to I-490 bridge: 2.8 miles

Estimated Time to Paddle: 2 hours round trip

Difficulty: ▶━◼ (minimal current)

Other Activities: Hike (3 major trails converge here: the Erie Canalway Trail, the Genesee Valley Greenway and the Genesee Riverway Trail)

Amenities: Genesee Waterways Center has a Porta-potty, playground and rents canoes & kayaks

Genesee Valley Park has trails, restrooms, and pavilions

Dogs: OK
Admission: Free
Field Contributor: Laura Arney
Contact: Genesee Waterways Center
149 Elmwood Avenue, Rochester, NY 14611
(585) 328-3960, www.geneseewaterways.org

Monroe County Parks Department
171 Reservoir Avenue, Rochester, NY 14620
(585) 256-4950, www.monroecounty.gov

Experience an easy paddle on three, successively smaller waterways, without the hassle of spotting a car at the end. You can launch from Genesee Waterways Center into the Genesee River or from the mouth of Red Creek and create your own round-trip using the Genesee River, Erie Canal and Red Creek. You can even paddle this section when the canal is drained. This segment retains water because of the Genesee River crossing.

Red Creek flows through Genesee Valley Golf Course.

In the wide Genesee River you can paddle downstream to the I-490 overpass in downtown Rochester. Below that is a dam. Upstream you could go a long ways—all the way to the Mt. Morris dam if your arms held out. Likewise, on the Erie Canal you could paddle west to Buffalo or east to Albany. Or, just putter around and explore the region where these two great waterways meet.

Red Creek is a mild-mannered flat-water stream through Genesee Valley Park, whose waters flow into the Erie Canal. Its minimal current makes it suitable for beginners. During high water you can paddle upstream past Crittenden Road.

Paddling Directions (up Red Creek):
- From the Genesee Waterways Center, head right, upstream on the Genesee River.
- Pass under the high, arched pedestrian bridge.
- Turn left into the Erie Canal and pass under a low, arched cement pedestrian bridge.
- Turn right into Red Creek and pass under the double I-390 bridges, then a low road bridge in Genesee Valley Park.
- Pass under an arched cement bridge in the golf course area of Genesee Valley Park, then the East River Road bridge.
- Reach the Crittenden Road bridge. When the water gets shallow, turn around and reverse the route.

Date visited:

Notes:

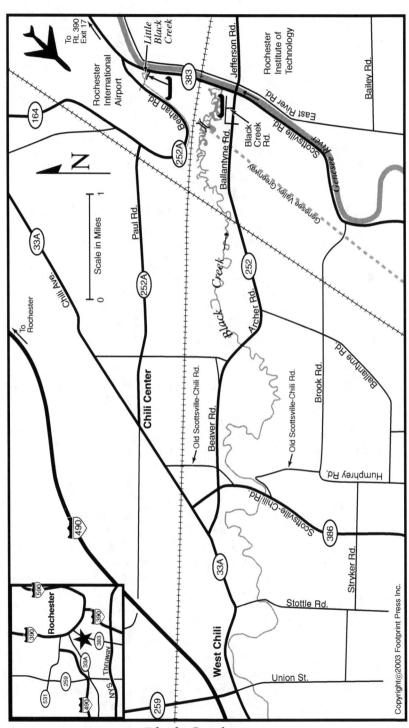

Black Creek (Chili)

8

BLACK CREEK
(Chili)

Location: Chili, Monroe County

Directions: From I-390 take exit 17 to Route 383 (Scottsville Road) heading south. Pass Route 252A. Turn right onto an unmarked road immediately before 84 Lumber for the Little Black Creek launch. For the Black Creek launch, continue south on Route 383, and turn right onto Route 252 (Ballantyne Road). After the ARC building, turn right onto Black Creek Road. At the end turn right, again on Black Creek Road. The launch area is on the left at the end of the road, marked by a brown and yellow DEC sign "Black Creek Fishing Access Site."

Little Black Creek Access Site: An 8-car parking area off Route 383 with picnic tables and a paved ramp (hand launch only) into the creek.

Black Creek Access Site: A large parking area off Black Creek Road with a Porta-potty, a paved boat ramp and dock and a gravel hand launch area.

Best Season to Visit: Summer or fall

Paddling Distance: Total: ~16 miles, round trip

Little Black Creek launch to Black Creek launch: 1 mile (45 minutes upstream, 15 minutes downstream)

Black Creek launch to tunnel under Genesee Valley Greenway: 0.5 mile

Tunnel to railroad bridge: 1.6 miles

Railroad bridge to Route 252: 2.0 miles

Route 252 to Route 386: 3.5 miles

Estimated Time to Paddle: Up Black Creek: 2-3 hours each way

Difficulty: ▬◖ ▬ ◖ (current in Genesee River, low arched tunnel to paddle through or portage over)

Other Activities: Fish, bird watch, hike the Genesee Valley Greenway Trail

Amenities: The Little Black Creek launch has picnic tables. The Black Creek launch has a Porta-potty.

Dogs:	OK
Admission:	Free
Contact:	DEC, Region 8
	6274 East Avon-Lima Road, Avon, NY 14414
	(585) 226-2466

Ah, the power of a chain saw and hard work! Every account we read about paddling upstream on Black Creek from the Genesee River mentioned that you couldn't go much farther than the railroad crossing before encountering downed trees and logjams. So, we headed out one summer morning expecting an easy but short paddle. We passed the railroad bridge and kept going, and going. We got almost to Route 386 before our energy waned and the stream got shallow. The entire route was wide open and evidence of chainsaw work abounded. We heard this was the handiwork of the Town of Chili. Thanks for a job well done, Chili!

You have several options for paddling this area. Launch and/or take-out into either Little Black Creek or Black Creek. There is current in the Genesee River, but it's easy to paddle upstream (and a fast return downstream). Little Black Creek is a narrow channel with water vegetation and islands of purple loosestrife. Explore the nooks and crannies, paddle under a low arched stone bridge and continue upstream a short distance before encountering logjams.

Black Creek is the prettier stream. It has no discernable current (in summer) and is wide and deep. You can paddle this area as a leisurely poke-about or go for distance. The lower stretches are dotted with islands and many side channels to explore. Paddle through a lush area with a remote feel, punctuated occasionally by a jet taking off from the nearby airport. The channel winds mercilessly. With no current, it can be a challenge to pick the main channel. When in doubt, select the widest channel with the least surface vegetation. The only obstacle is the low, arched, stone tunnel under what is now the Genesee Valley Greenway Trail. We were able to paddle under it. (Rich had to duck, but Sue didn't.) If water level or your tolerance for confined spaces dictates, you can portage over it from the left bank. We saw evidence of tree stubs chewed by beavers and watched a kingfisher leave a tree and dive head-first into the water on a fishing spree. The banks were ablaze in yellow flowers and in the red of cardinal flower - unusual to see in its native habitat.

For a more strenuous paddle, follow the main channel and see how far you can get before you run out of energy or water (shallow). There is no access from the bridges of Routes 252 and 386. Upstream of the railroad bridge, the noises of civilization disappear. After the Route 252 bridge, you'll begin to discern a current and the banks will become muddy.

Paddling Directions (between launches):

- From the Little Black Creek launch (off Route 383) head left to explore upstream. You may have to push through downed trees and brush.
- Shortly, reach a low, arched, stone tunnel under an abandoned railway. If it's passable, paddle through it, otherwise turn around. (Past the tunnel you'll paddle under the Beahan Road bridge then down a winding channel only a short way before reaching a logjam.) Return down Little Black Creek.
- Continue downstream, under the cement Route 383 bridge to the Genesee River and head right, upstream.
- Paddle under an active, but rusted railroad trestle.
- Turn right and paddle under a green highway bridge into wide Black Creek.
- Bear left to the Black Creek access site.

Paddling Directions (upstream on Black Creek):

- From the DEC launch, head left, upstream. Explore around islands and into side channels at will. The main channel will be wide and have the least duckweed and seaweed.
- Paddle through the arched, stone tunnel under the Genesee Valley Greenway or portage from the left bank.
- Pass under the high cement bridge with green, red and silver rails. This is an active rail line.
- Pass a wide channel to your right.
- Paddle under the green Route 252 highway bridge.
- Turnaround whenever you get tired or no longer want to paddle against the shallow water or current.
- Return downstream to either launch.

Date visited:

Notes:

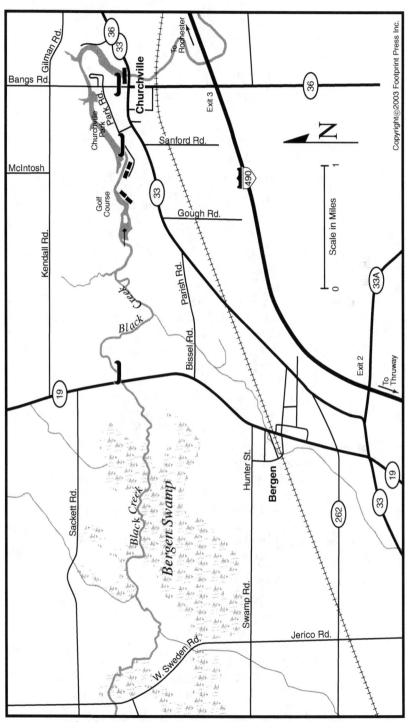

Black Creek (Route 19 to Churchville Dam)

9

BLACK CREEK
(Route 19 to Churchville Dam)

Location: Bergen and Churchville, Genesee & Monroe Counties

Directions: From I-490 take exit 2 and follow Routes 33A then 33 west to Route 19. Turn north onto Route 19 through Bergen. Park at the northeast corner of the bridge over Black Creek at the end of the guardrail.

Launch Site #1: From the northeast corner of the Route 19 bridge follow the grass path 200 yards to a rocky slope to put in downstream, left.

Launch Site #2: From Route 36 (Main Street, Churchville) turn west on Park Road into Churchville Park. Bear right when the road bends then follow signs to the canoe launch. You'll find parking for 10 cars and a sloped gravel ramp.

Take-out Site: From Route 33 in Churchville you can find parking and a take-out bank above the dam on either side. The largest parking area is on the east side of the creek across from the Churchville Fire Department.

Best Season to Visit: Summer or fall

Paddling Distance: Total: 4.3 miles
Route 19 to Churchville Park launch: 2.8 miles (1 hour)
Churchville Park to the dam: 1.5 miles (0.5 hour)

Estimated Time to Paddle: 1.5 - 2 hours in July (one way)

Difficulty:

Other Activities: Fish, bird watch

Amenities: Churchville Park has shelters, playgrounds and restrooms but not near the launch

Dogs: OK on leash in the park

Admission: Free

Contact: Monroe County Parks Department
171 Reservoir Avenue, Rochester, NY 14620
(585) 256-4950, www.monroecounty.gov

The dam in Churchville creates a backwater that's deep enough to paddle even in summer. At Route 19 we found 4-foot-deep water in a narrow channel that widened the further downstream we went. Blowdowns had been cleared, creating an easy passage. The channel is open to the powers of the sun, so wear sunscreen. You could easily put in at one of the other two access sites and paddle this area as a round trip.

There's a very nice launch site upstream at the West Sweden Road bridge, which puts you floating down Black Creek through Bergen Swamp. It sounds like fun—a nice idyllic ride through pristine forests for 3.7 miles to Route 19. Indeed, one early July day it was a gorgeous paddle through a narrow, winding channel in what felt like a primeval forest. The problem was that after 20 portages we hadn't made it even one mile downstream. So, banish thoughts about starting farther upstream unless you're excited about the prospect of portaging every 30 feet through waist deep nettles that send knife-like barbs into your skin and lush stands of poison ivy that leave reminders long after the nettle stings have vanished.

In all fairness, we've read that other people have paddled this section in previous years. At times someone clears the logjams through the swamp. If it was cleared, it would be a beautiful route (3.7 miles from West Sweden Road to Route 19). Heed our warning though, and paddle it upstream first so you can turn around if you encounter the mess of logjams that blocked passage in 2003.

Paddling Directions:
- From Route 19 head downstream.
- Paddle around islands and explore the cattail-lined side channels.
- Pass a golf course (part of Churchville Park) on the left and houses on the right.
- The channel will widen, becoming pond-like.
- Watch for the Churchville Park hand launch to the right.
- Pass under the pretty, arched, cement bridge of Route 36.
- The dam is upstream of the Route 33 bridge (a brown highway bridge). Pull-out left or right, well upstream of the dam.

Date visited:

Notes:

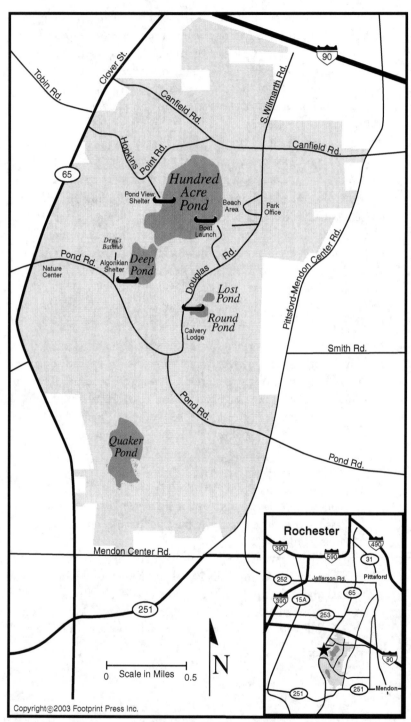

Mendon Ponds

10

MENDON

Location: Mendon Ponds Park, Monroe County

Directions: From I-90 take exit 46 and head east on Lehigh Station Road. At the end turn south on Route 65 (Clover Street). To find the official boat launch, turn east into Mendon Ponds Park on Canfield Road then south onto Douglas Road. Pass signs for the beach area then turn right at the sign for the boat launch.

Launch & Take-out Site #1: The official boat launch has a large gravel parking area next to a sand beach, the shore of Hundred Acre Pond.

Launch & Take-out Site #2: Another access point for Hundred Acre Pond is across the pond at Pond View Shelter. From the large parking area it's a 50-yard carry to the sand beach.

Launch & Take-out Site #3: The most scenic launch is at Algonkian Shelter off Pond Road. This puts you on a small beach into a lily and cattail side arm of Deep Pond. There's room to park 10 cars.

Launch & Take-out Site #4: There's a 3-car parking area next to Round Pond off Douglas Road with a gravel beach access.

Best Season to Visit: Spring & early summer (can get weed choked by late summer)

Paddling Distance: It's almost a mile from the top of Hundred Acre Pond to the bottom of Deep Pond. They're connected by an easy-to-portage dirt dike.

Estimated Time to Paddle: An hour or two

Difficulty: ▶━━■ (more difficult if winds are strong)

Other Activities: Bird watch, hike, picnic, swim

Amenities: The park offers picnic tables, grills, rest rooms and an extensive network of hiking trails.

Dogs: OK on leash

Admission: Free

Contact: Monroe County Parks Department
171 Reservoir Avenue, Rochester, NY 14620
(585) 256-4950, www.monroecounty.gov/org

The channel into Deep Pond from Algonkian Shelter
in Mendon Ponds Park.

This is a jewel in the Monroe County Park system, filled with lakes, woods, and rolling hills. Mendon Ponds Park is the largest park in Monroe County and was designated a National Natural Landmark because of its unique glacial land forms.

The park's geologic features were formed by the last of four major glaciers that covered the area 12,000 to 14,000 years ago. The glacier reached to the Pennsylvania border and was 5,000 to 10,000 feet thick. As the ice melted, large amounts of sand, rock, and gravel were deposited. The three main geologic features visible in the park today are kames, eskers, and kettles.

The first inhabitants of this area were the Algonquin, Iroquois, and Seneca Indians who left behind many trails. In 1687, the Marquis de Denonville's army used the trails to attack the Indians in the region. In his memoirs, Denonville recalls looking down from the top of one of the ridges at "three pretty little lakes." It's the first reference to Mendon Ponds in our recorded history. The first white settler in the Mendon Ponds area was Joshua Lillie, who is buried on a small plot on Wilmarth Road. The park was dedicated in 1928 and now has 25 to 30 miles of winding trails and 8 ponds, 4 of which can be paddled.

Every spring the Adirondack Mountain Club holds an
Outdoor Expo at Mendon Ponds where you can try boats
and attend workshops for free.

The ponds are great for family outings and for anyone learning to
paddle. All access points are via sand beaches. Hundred Acre Pond
covers 120 acres and is attached to 30-acre Deep Pond by a culvert
covered by an earthen dam. Sometimes you can paddle through the
culvert; other times it's an easy portage over the earthen dam. Deep
Pond is misnamed. It is rather shallow, with edges lined in cattails,
yellow pond lilies, fragrant white water lilies and arrowhead. The
ponds are lush with birds, including many year-round resident
Canada geese.

Round and Lost Ponds are much smaller, but they're scenic and
you're likely to have them to yourself. They're definitely worth
exploring. One paddler recommends that you take a book and let
the breezes push your canoe or kayak to unexplored areas of these
ponds. By all means, take your binoculars.

Paddling Directions:
  • Explore the various ponds at will.

Date visited:

Notes:

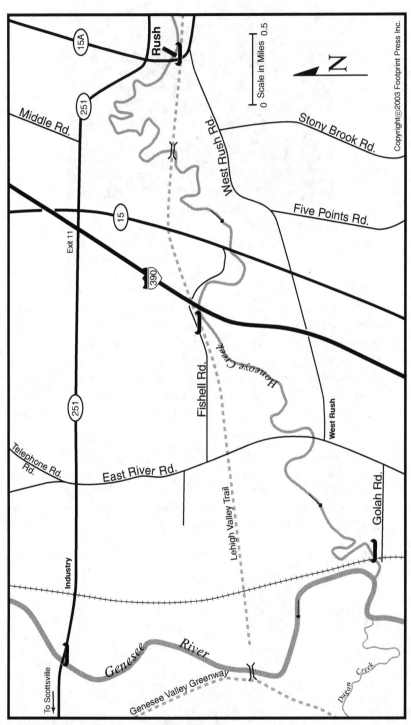

Honeoye Creek and Genesee River (Rush to Scottsville)

11

HONEOYE CREEK & GENESEE RIVER
(Rush to Scottsville)

Location: Rush and Wheatland, Monroe County

Directions: From I-390 take exit 11 and head east on Route 251. Turn right on Route 15A (E. Henrietta Road) into Rush. Cross over the Honeoye Creek bridge and immediately turn left into Rush Veterans Memorial Park. Park along the split rail fence.

Launch Site #1: In Rush Veterans Memorial Park, carry across the grass and down a dirt path (50 yards) behind the flag pole to put in below the dam.

Launch Site #2: Under the I-390 bridge off Fishell Road is a large parking area marked with a DEC sign "Honeoye Creek Fishing Access Site." Access to the creek is via a muddy slope.

Launch Site #3: From East River Road turn west onto unlabeled, dead-end Golah Road. Park after the substation, just before the railroad tracks in the large grass area. A 15-yard carry leads to an easy access site upstream, left.

Take-out Site: On the southeast side of the Route 251 Genesee River bridge is a 10-car parking area labeled "Genesee River Fishing Access Site." Cement steps lead 25 yards to water's edge.

Best Season to Visit: Summer or fall

Paddling Distance: Total: 11.3 miles
Route 15A to Fishell Road: 4.4 miles (1.5 hrs.)
Fishell Road to Golah Road: 3.6 miles (1.5 hrs.)
Golah Road to Route 251: 3.3 miles (1 hour)

Estimated Time to Paddle: 4 hours in July

Difficulty:

(expect portages, minimal current in July)

Water Level Information: http://waterdata.usgs.gov/ny/nwis/rt
(the gage, # 04229500, is significantly upstream
of this segment, at Honeoye Falls)

Other Activities: Fish, bird watch

Amenities: Rush Veterans Memorial Park has a gazebo, grills
and benches

Dogs: OK

Admission: Free

Contact: DEC, Region 8
6274 East Avon-Lima Road, Avon, NY 14414
(585) 226-2466

Honeoye Creek was a clear-water stream lined in sand and seaweed by mid-July. There are lots of twists in the channel and small islands around which to paddle. We had to do 5 easy portages to get around downed trees and logjams. You'll paddle through the greenery of grass banks and arrowhead plants. We repeatedly saw deer standing in the waterway, getting a summer drink.

The Genesee River is wide and deep, in high mud banks, with no discernable current in July. It's easy padding to the take-out.

Paddling Directions:

- From Rush Veterans Memorial Park, head downstream under the silver-railed Route 15A bridge.
- Watch for logjams. You will probably have to portage.
- Pass under a railroad bridge which now carries the Lehigh Valley Trail.
- Pass under the silver-railed Route 15 bridge then through some shallow areas.
- Under the I-390 bridge on the right is the mud bank of launch site #2.
- Pass under the brown East River Road highway bridge.
- Upstream, left of the railroad bridge is the access point for Golah Road. Paddle under the railroad trestle.
- One final easy portage to endure.
- When the water turns muddy and mud banks line the shore you know you're nearing the Genesee River.
- Turn right into the wide Genesee River and paddle downstream.

- Pass under the abandoned railroad trestle. (Some day this will connect the Lehigh Valley Trail to the Genesee Valley Greenway Trail.)
- Take out at the cement steps on the right below the Route 251 bridge (upstream, right).

Date visited:

Notes:

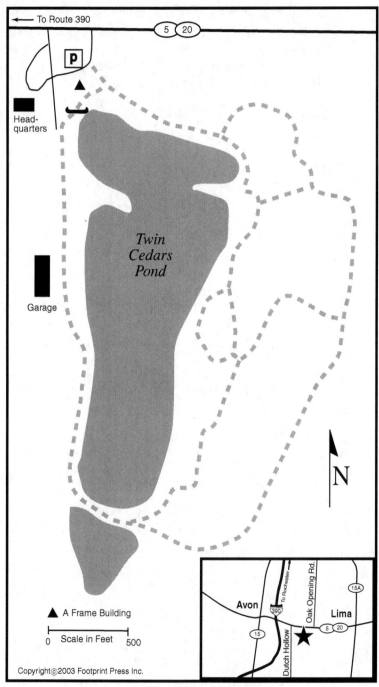

To Route 390

5 20

P

Head-
quarters

Garage

*Twin
Cedars
Pond*

N

▲ A Frame Building

0   Scale in Feet   500

Copyright©2003 Footprint Press Inc.

Avon

To Rochester

Oak Opening Rd.

390

15A

Lima

15

Dutch Hollow

5 20

Twin Cedars Pond

12

TWIN CEDARS POND

Location: Twin Cedars Environmental Area, East Avon,
                        Livingston County

Directions: Twin Cedars Environmental Area is at the DEC
                        Region 8 Headquarters on the south side of
                        Routes 5 & 20, east of I-390. Pull into the head
                        quarters at the brown sign "NYS DEC Region 8
                        Headquarters" and bear left to park near the red
                        A-frame building.

Launch & Take-out Site: From the visitor parking area near the A-
                        frame, it's a 100 yard carry across grass to a short
                        grass bank at the northwest corner of the pond.

Best Season to Visit: Summer (avoid spring nesting season)

Paddling Distance: The pond is 0.3 mile long

Estimated Time to Paddle: 0.5 to 2 hours

Difficulty: ▶━━━●

Other Activities: Fish, bird watch, hike

Amenities: Picnic tables and hiking on a 1-mile outer loop or
                        a 0.7 mile inner loop trail

Dogs: OK on leash

Admission: Free

Contact: DEC, Region 8
                        6274 East Avon-Lima Road, Avon, NY 14414
                        (585) 226-2466

Twin Cedars Environmental Area began in 1970 when DEC purchased some farmland adjacent to its offices. In 1974, DEC purchased another 59 acres and enlarged the pond, using an earthen dike to impound naturally flowing water. In the 1980s, the area was developed into an educational area, designed to emphasize the natural and man-made aspects of environmental conservation.

The A-frame building serves as an interpretive center. It is loaded with stuffed animals, an extensive collection of bird eggs, along with live fish and turtles. The exhibits and displays are designed to test visitors' environmental knowledge and to stimulate their curiosity. It is open year-round, most weekdays from 8:00 AM until 4:30 PM.

Call ahead to make sure the interpretive center is open to the public on the day of your visit. The pond and trails are open any time.

The pond has convoluted shores rimmed with trees and fields and a maximum depth of 15 feet. In the pond you'll find goose nesting platforms, wood duck boxes (on poles), waterfowl nesting tripods (man-made nests suspended over water by metal tripods), nesting rafts (used for nesting by Canada geese and grebes and for sunning by turtles), and a bat house. The pond has been stocked with largemouth bass, black crappie, bluegills, pumpkinseeds, and tiger muskies. In 1993, triploid grass carp were added as a biological agent to control aquatic vegetation. Fishing is permitted with a valid license. Any triploid grass carp caught must be returned to the pond.

Paddling Directions:
   • Explore the pond at will.

   Date visited:

   Notes:

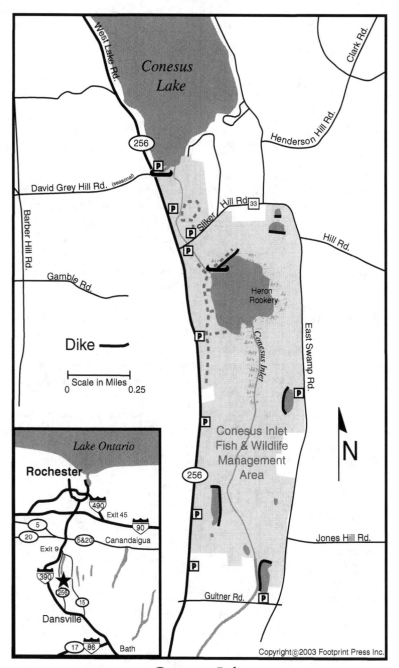

Conesus Inlet

13

CONESUS INLET

Location: Conesus Inlet Fish and Wildlife Management Area, south end of Conesus Lake, Livingston County

Directions: Take I-390 to Route 15 (Conesus Lake exit). Then head south on Route 15 to Route 256. Head south on Route 256 past the lake about 0.5 mile to Sliker Hill Road. Turn left on Sliker Hill Road then right at the green "Welcome to Conesus" sign, into the DEC parking lot.

Launch Site #1: A DEC parking area on the south side of Sliker Hill Road. There's a 100-yard carry past the yellow metal gate to put in above the dike.

Launch Site #2: At the South end of Conesus Lake where the inlet meets the lake, off Route 256 is a DEC "Conesus Lake Fishing Access Site" parking area with room for 40 cars and a sloped gravel, hand boat launch. (Provides access to Conesus Lake but not to the WMA.)

Best Season to Visit: Spring and early summer (dense vegetation can make paddling difficult by late summer)

Paddling Distance: About 2 miles round trip

Estimated Time to Paddle: An hour or more, depending on how much exploring you do

Difficulty: ▶━━ (more if the wind is strong)

Other Activities: Fish, bird watch, hike (a 0.5-mile trail leads south from the parking area)

Amenities: None

Dogs: OK

Admission: Free

Contact: DEC, Region 8
6274 East Avon-Lima Road, Avon, NY 14414
(585) 226-2466

An easy paddle among the dead trees of Conesus Inlet.

Conesus Lake is a very popular and heavily used lake that supports a cottage community. There is a lot of activity on the lake and immediate waterfront year-round.

The Conesus Inlet Fish and Wildlife Management Area is a marsh at the south end of the lake that covers over 1,168 acres. The DEC purchased the land in the late 1960s and initiated wildlife programs to conserve and protect this vital wetland resource. In 1979 an additional 83 acres were added to provide boat access to the lake, and preserve critical pike spawning habitat. The latest purchase was 48 acres in 2001.

The Conesus Inlet is a waterway that winds through the marsh and drains water from the surrounding hills into Conesus Lake. A long earthen dike creates a large, shallow pond that's dotted with grass islands and stumps of dead trees. Since the water is shallow, water plants proliferate by late summer and you may have to pole through some of the marsh. In spring and early summer it's a magnificent place to paddle for bird watching, especially since there's a heron rookery at the southeast corner of the pond. Look for a cluster of large nests high in the trees. Please do not disturb the rookery. The wildlife is abundant wherever you choose to paddle.

Paddling Directions:
- From the Sliker Hill Road parking lot carry your canoe or kayak (100 yards) past the yellow metal gates and take the first left to the dike to launch.
- Paddle wherever you want in the pond.

Date visited:

Notes:

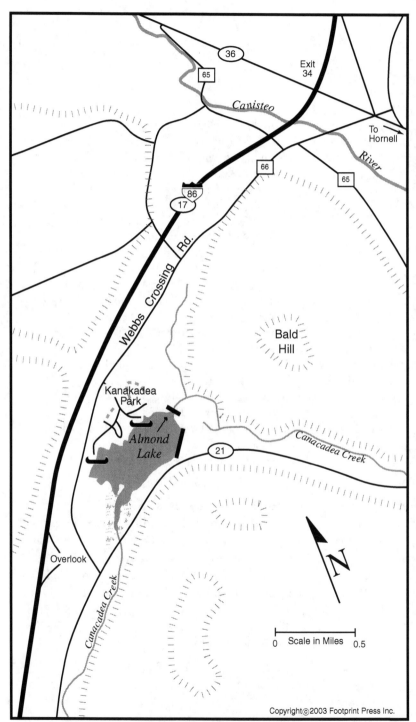

Almond Lake

14

ALMOND LAKE

Location: Hornell, Steuben County

Directions: From I-86 (old Route 17) take exit 34, west of Hornell, and follow Route 36 south. Turn right (W) onto County Route 66. Kanakadea Park entrance, marked by a big green and white sign, is 2.5 mile on the left.

Launch Site #1: Straight back on the park entrance road is a paved, sloped ramp into the water.

Launch Site #2: At the west end of the camping area is a sloped dirt launch area.

Best Season to Visit: Spring, summer and fall

Nearby Campgrounds: Kanakadea Park offers camping April 15 - Oct. 1

Paddling Distance: Almond Lake is 0.75 mile long

Estimated Time to Paddle: 1 to 2 hours

Difficulty: ▬▬◄█

Other Activities: Fish, hike, sports fields, playgrounds, camp

Amenities: Picnic areas, restrooms

Dogs: OK on leash under 6 feet long

Admission: Free, park closes at 9 PM

Contact: Steuben County Dept. of Public Works, Parks Dept.
Kanakadea Park
7268 Web Crossing Road, Hornell
(607) 324-0539

A scenic overlook on I-86 between exits 33 and 34, heading east, gives a bird's-eye view of Almond Lake and its dam. Placid Almond Lake was formed by damming Canacadea Creek as part of the flood control plan for the communities of southern New York. The dike has a steep gravel bank, but the other shores are grass or tree lined. At the western end is a marsh in which you can poke around. This lake is family-friendly, especially because of Kanakadea Park that sits on the northeast shore. It offers camping and typical park facilities that provide the variety that families need.

Date visited:

Notes:

Paddles in Allegany, Cattaraugus and Chautauqua Counties

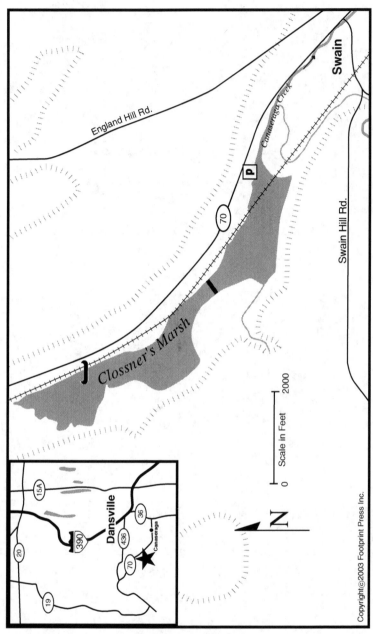

Clossner's Marsh

15

CLOSSNER'S MARSH

Location: Swain, Allegany County

Directions: From I-390 take exit 4 (Dansville) and turn right onto Route 36. Head south, then turn right onto Route 70. Continue through Canaseraga, Garwoods and Swain. The parking area is on the left (south side) about 2 miles past Swain, next to the railroad, marked with a white sign "State of NY DEC Wildlife Area Rules & Regulations." It's the second dirt parking area after Swain. The first doesn't have water access.

Launch Site #1: From the parking area carry your boat 35 yards down a dirt path on the right. The launch area is a dirt bank.

Best Season to Visit: Spring, summer and fall

Paddling Distance: The pond is 1.8 miles long
Launch to north end is 0.3 mile
Launch to the dike is 0.7 mile
Dike to SE end of pond is 0.8 mile

Estimated Time to Paddle: 2 to 3 hours

Difficulty: ▸━━

Other Activities: Fish, bird watch

Amenities: None

Dogs: OK

Admission: Free

Contact: DEC, Region 9
5425 County Route 48, Belmont, NY 14813
(585) 268-5392
www.dec.state.ny.us

Clossner's Marsh is the headwaters of Canaseraga Creek. The creek itself is too shallow to paddle, even in spring, but the pond of Clossner's Marsh provides 1.8 miles to paddle. Lots of ducks and geese make this pond home. In the middle of the pond is an earthen dike (a private drive) that can be easily portaged over to access the southern reaches of the pond. In springtime you'll find people fishing for bullheads.

Paddling Directions:
- From the launch area, duck under the low railroad bridge (2.5 feet clearance) to reach the lily-filled pond.
- Paddle anywhere you want in the pond.

Date visited:

Notes:

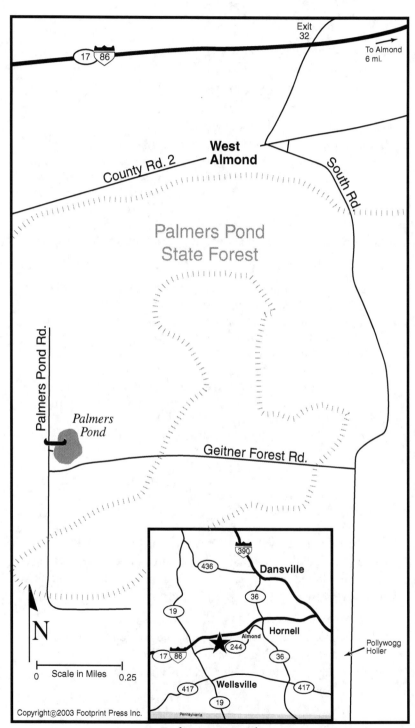

Palmers Pond

16

PALMERS POND

Location: West Almond, Allegany County
Directions: From I-86 (old Route 17) take exit 32 (West Almond) and head south on County Road 2 into West Almond. Take the first left onto South Road. Turn right onto Geitner Forest Road. Turn right onto Palmers Pond Road and watch for the parking area on the right.
Launch Site #1: Close to the parking area, the launch is a grassy pond edge
Best Season to Visit: Spring, summer and fall
Nearby Campgrounds: Primitive campsites are available along the pond shore. Camping is also allowed in the section of Palmers Pond State Forest north of I-86.
Paddling Distance: 0.3 mile around the pond
Estimated Time to Paddle: 0.5 hour or more
Difficulty:
Other Activities: Hike (Palmers Pond and Phillips Creek State Forests are criss-crossed with a network of trails)
Amenities: Porta-potty, picnic table
Dogs: OK
Admission: Free
Contact: DEC, Region 9
5425 County Route 48, Belmont, NY 14813
(585) 268-5392
www.dec.state.ny.us

Rough dirt roads will lead you to this oasis in the forest. Palmers Pond is a small (4-acre), placid, rust-colored pond nestled in a pine forest. It's dotted with at least 5 small islands to putter around. Pack a lunch and enjoy a day appreciating nature. Just don't feed the resident geese.

For a unique experience, visit Pollywogg Hollër Eco-Resort at 6242 South Road. It's a rustic lodge tucked in the woods among eclectic sculptures created by the students from Alfred State College.

Canada geese enjoy the quiet of secluded Palmers Pond.

The lodge buildings vary from a loft over a wood-fired sauna to a rustic log cabin, each built lovingly by owner Bill Castle and his family. (800-291-9668, www.pollywoggholler.com)

Paddling Directions:
   • Explore at will.

Date visited:

Notes:

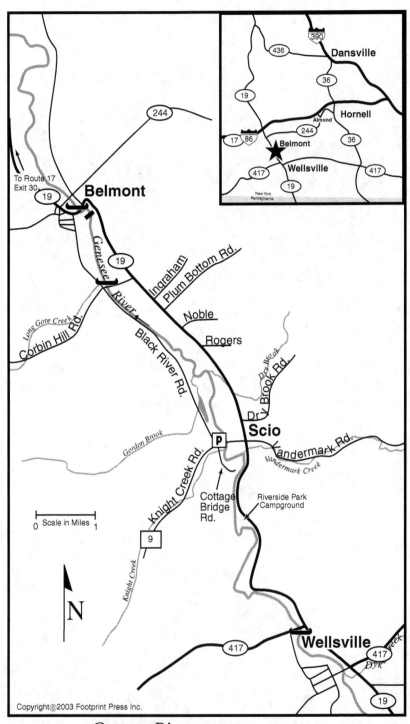

Genesee River (Wellsville to Belmont)

17

GENESEE RIVER
(Wellsville to Belmont)

Location: Wellsville, Scio and Belmont, Allegany County

Directions: From I-86 (old Route 17) exit at Belvidere and head south on Route 19. In Wellsville, turn right onto Route 417 West. Quickly cross the Genesee River and park in the Tops/K-Mart parking lot along the river.

Launch Site: From the north end of the Route 417 Tops/K-Mart parking lot, it's a short carry down a grassy bank to a level launch area.

Take-out Site: In Belmont, parking is on Route 19 (Schuyler Street) on the east side of the river, across from the Belmont Fire Department and Carpets Unlimited (near the corner of Greenwich & Schuyler Streets). Do not park in front of the fire hydrant. The launch is a short dirt bank. There is a 10-foot-high arched dam just south of Route 19 in Belmont.

Best Season to Visit: Spring, summer and fall (check water gage before heading out)

Nearby Campgrounds: Riverside Park Campground, 3549 Riverside Drive, Wellsville, NY 14895 (585) 593-3856, www.netsos.com/rs/riverpark.html
Park Meadow Campground, RD1 Ingraham Road, Belmont (585) 268-7340

Paddling Distance: 10 miles (dropping 10 feet per mile)

Estimated Time to Paddle: 3 hours

Difficulty: (ripples and some downed trees)

Water Level Information: http://waterdata.usgs.gov/ny/nwis/rt (the gage is at the start in Wellsville, #04221000) http://205.156.54.206/er/buf/products/BUFRVD BUF1.html (check the 7 AM Stage for Genesee River - Wellsville. This segment is not navigable if it's below 4.5)

Other Activities: Fish, bird watch

A kayaker approaches from above the Belmont Dam,
the end of this segment on the Genesee River.

Amenities: Belmont has a food mart and pizza shop
Dogs: OK
Admission: Free
Field Contributor: Laura Arney

This stretch of the Genesee River is a rush for novices. We paddled it in late July with low water levels and had to push over shallow spots quite often. Even in late July the current was swift and the stream was a constant series of ripples and small runs interspersed with flat water sections. We could almost always see a clear run out beyond the ripples which calmed my inexperienced, wildly beating heart. A few times we walked the kayaks around chutes that were impeded by trees or where we couldn't see the run out before a pull-out decision had to be made. This is not flat water, but it is a great place to try your first run at small ripples. The water would be higher in spring and probably cover many of the ripples. Others might turn into class II white water. Just avoid heavy spring run off time—the Genesee River can be powerful during spring run-off—even these southerly stretches.

Expect some road noise while you're near Route 19, but you'll encounter few signs of civilization. The view is of wooded banks and a few sharply cut sand banks for variety. Your companions will be ducks, herons, crows, and woodchucks, unless you take a rowdy bunch of humans with you.

You may encounter people fishing—the upper Genesee is prime trout water. Trout flourish in the cool water and some low-water dams (that you'll float over unnoticed) near Belmont create pools for the fish.

The water level is gaged daily on the Genesee River. Log onto http://205.156.54.206/er/buf/products/BUFRVDBUF1.html to check the 7 AM Stage for Genesee River - Wellsville. This segment is not navigable if it's below 4.5.

The Genesee River is the longest river in Western New York State and the third longest in the entire state. It is one of only a few major rivers in the USA to flow north. The Genesee starts in Pennsylvania as springs in a farmer's field and runs north through Letchworth Gorge and Rochester to Lake Ontario. There is a huge flood control dam at Mt. Morris at the north end of Letchworth Gorge and major waterfalls in both Letchworth and Rochester.

The river south of Wellsville is not for novices. It's too shallow to run, except at high water levels when the current is fast. It also has sharp bends that can be blocked by downed trees, and it's riddled with low dams and dikes. In Wellsville the channels and cement bed were put in place after the devastating flood of 1950. In Belmont there is a dam then some ledges (waterfalls) before the river flattens out again. See page 92 for information on paddling downstream from Belmont.

Paddling Directions:
- From Wellsville, head downstream.
- Pass under a grate bridge for the golf course.
- There will be lots of small sections of ripples. Route 19 parallels the river on your right so you will hear some road noise.
- Pass Riverside Park Campground on your right.
- A farm house on the left marks the end of Cottage Bridge Road.
- Vandermark Creek (a strong stream) comes in from the right.
- See railroad crossing signs and the old metal railroad bridge on the right as you approach Scio.
- Pass under the County Route 9 bridge. (There is access under the bridge, right, but it's a steep rocky climb to parking at a DEC fishing access site.)

- Knight Creek comes in from the left.
- Gordon Brook comes in from the left.
- Black River Road now parallels the river on your left.
- Pass Corbin Hill Road (Route 31A) bridge. (Good access under bridge, right to a sloped pull-out with a 150-foot carry across grass to a DEC fishing access parking lot.)
- When you see the bridge in Belmont, hug the right bank. You won't see the dam. Bear right into a stagnant channel to the parking area.

Date visited:

Notes:

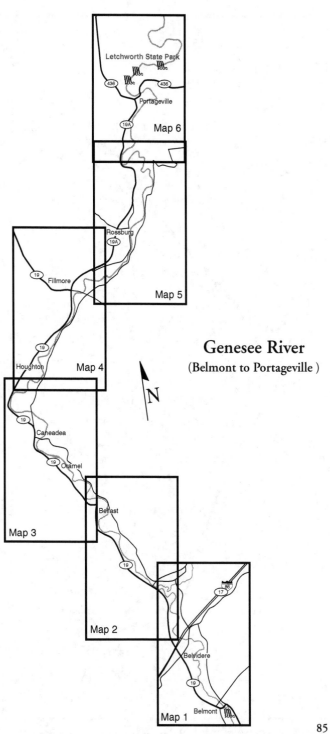

Letchworth State Park

436 436

Portageville

19A

Map 6

Rossburg
19A

19 Fillmore

Map 5

Genesee River
(Belmont to Portageville)

19

N

Houghton **Map 4**

19 Caneadea

19 Oramel

Belfast

Map 3

19

86
17

Map 2

Belvidere

19

Map 1 Belmont

85

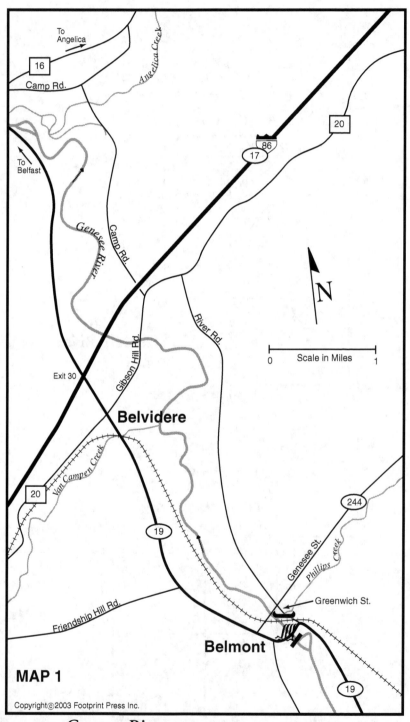

Genesee River (Belmont to Portageville - Map 1)

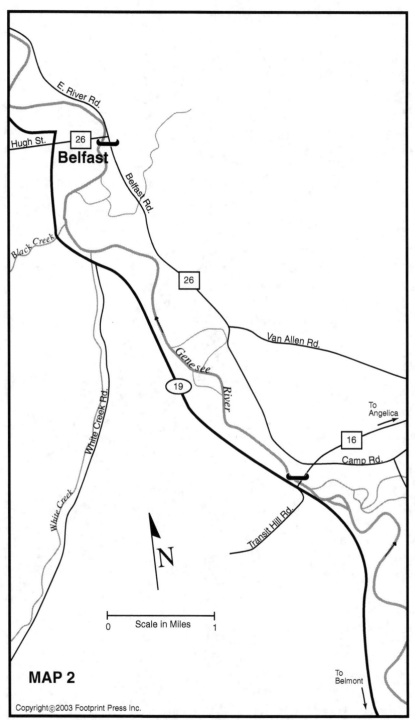

MAP 2

Genesee River (Belmont to Portageville - Map 2)

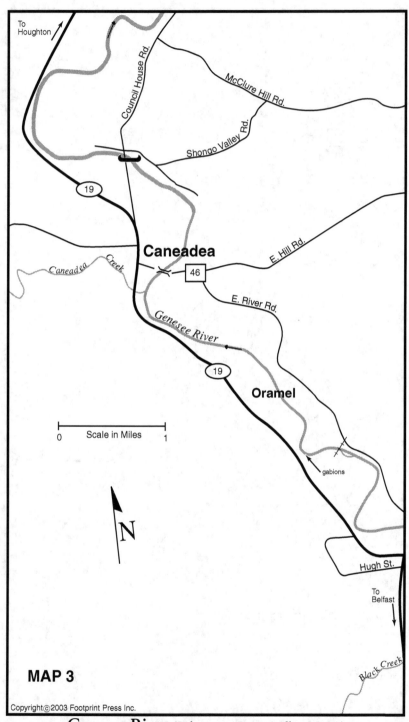

To
Houghton

Council House Rd.

McClure Hill Rd.

Shongo Valley Rd.

19

Caneadea

Caneadea Creek

E. Hill Rd.

46

E. River Rd.

Genesee River

19

Oramel

0 Scale in Miles 1

gabions

N

Hugh St.

To
Belfast

Black Creek

MAP 3

Copyright©2003 Footprint Press Inc.

Genesee River (Belmont to Portageville - Map 3)

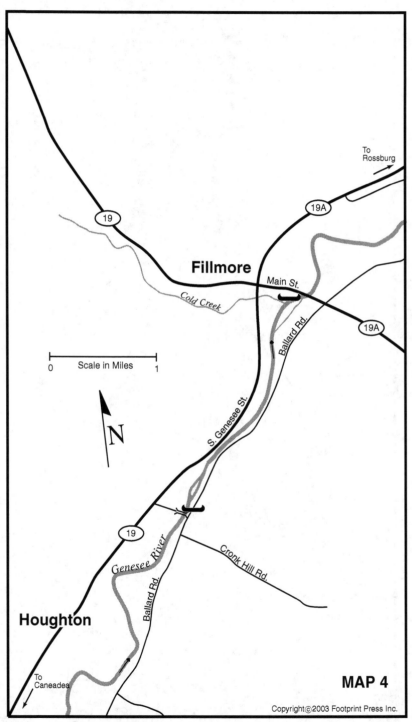

To
Rossburg

19

19A

Fillmore

Main St.

Cold Creek

Ballard Rd.

19A

Scale in Miles
0   1

N

S. Genesee St.

19

Genesee River

Cronk Hill Rd.

Houghton

Ballard Rd.

To
Caneadea

MAP 4

Copyright©2003 Footprint Press Inc.

Genesee River (Belmont to Portageville - Map 4)

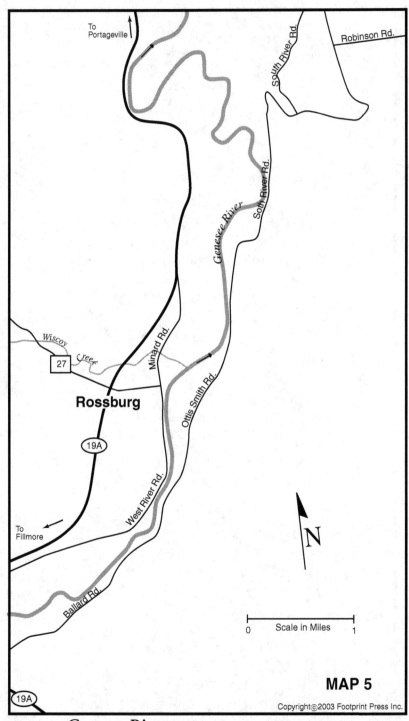

To Portageville

Robinson Rd.

South River Rd.

Soth River Rd.

Genesee River

Wiscoy Creek

27

Minard Rd.

Rossburg

19A

Ottis Smith Rd.

West River Rd.

To Fillmore

N

Ballard Rd.

0   Scale in Miles   1

MAP 5

Copyright©2003 Footprint Press Inc.

19A

Genesee River (Belmont to Portageville - Map 5)

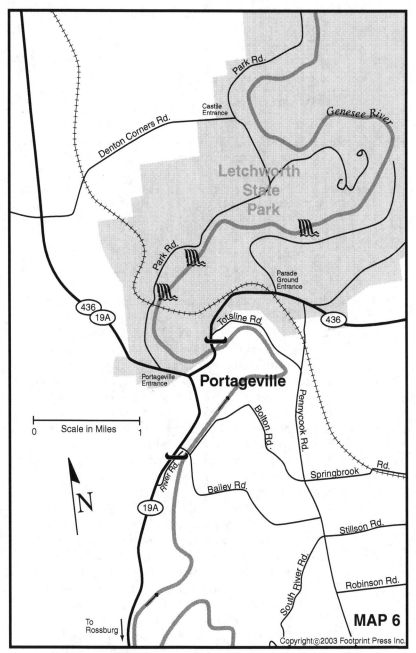

Genesee River (Belmont to Portageville - Map 6)

18

GENESEE RIVER
(Belmont to Portageville)

Location: Belmont, Belfast, Caneadea, Houghton, Fillmore and Portageville in Allegany and Livingston Counties

Directions: From I-86 take exit 30 (Belmont) and head south on Route 19. In Belmont turn east onto Route 244 (Genesee Street) then south onto Greenwich Street. Cross over the Phillips Creek bridge and take an immediate right onto a dirt road at the Laidlaw factory building. The dirt road leads to water level.

Launch Site # 1: From the gravel road next to Phillips Creek in Belmont there's a level gravel beach for launching.

Access Site # 2: County Road 16, west of Angelica has parking for 3 cars at the east side of the bridge and an old dirt road leading 200 yards to water level.

Access Site # 3: In Belfast there's a large parking area on the SE corner of County Route 26 and Hugh Street. An old dirt road leads down 150 yards to water level.

Access Site # 4: North of Caneadea there's a dirt road off the south side of the Council House Road bridge (a.k.a. Lattice Bridge Road) that leads to a muddy shore, upstream, left.

Access Site # 5: North of Caneadea, Council House Road turns into Ballard Road. Just past Cronk Hill Road park on the left at the bridge-closed barrier. A dirt path leads down to the rocks below the bridge.

Access Site # 6: In Fillmore take Main Street (Route 19A) east. Before the bridge over the Genesee River a large parking area will be on the right. In dry weather you can drive down to the flat gravel river shore, otherwise it's a 50-yard carry.

Access Site # 7: South of Portageville take River Road off Route 19A. This dirt road leads to a dirt slope below the high, brown highway bridge of Bolton Road.

Final Take-out Site: Take Route 436 east through Portageville and cross over the Genesee River. Immediately after the bridge on the northeast side, at the corner of Totsline Road, is a parking area and a path leading 50 yards to upstream, right of the bridge. The bridge has 4 large cement arches. Waterfalls begin downstream from this bridge.

Best Season to Visit: Late spring (check water gage before heading out)

Nearby Campgrounds: Six-S Campground, 5920 County Road 16, Belfast, NY 14711, (716) 365-2201

Letchworth State Park, 1 Letchworth State Park, Castile, NY 14427, (585) 493-3600, http://nysparks.state.ny.us/parks/

Paddling Distance: 40.4 miles (Belfast to Portageville)

Belmont to County Road 16: 8.2 miles (2 hours)

County Road 16 to County Route 26: 4.7 miles (1 hour)

County Route 26 to Council House Road: 6.5 Miles (1.5 hours)

Council House Road to closed bridge: 4.9 miles (1.25 hours)

Closed bridge to Route 19A: 2.6 miles (1 hour)

Route 19A to River Road: 11.3 miles (3 hours)

River Road to Route 436: 2.2 miles (0.5 hour)

Estimated Time to Paddle: 7 to 8 hours (Belmont to Fillmore)

Difficulty: (from Belmont to Fillmore - lots of ripples, small white-water, fast chutes and some downed trees, but tough spots can be easily portaged around; there may be strainers)

(from Fillmore to Portageville)

Water Level Information: http://waterdata.usgs.gov/ny/nwis/rt (gage #04223000 is at the end in Portageville, also check gage #04221000 which is upstream in Wellsville) http://205.156.54.206/er/buf/products/BUFRVD BUF1.html

Other Activities: Fish, bird watch

Amenities: Belmont has a food mart and pizza shop.
The Belvidere Restaurant near the crossing of Routes 20 and 19, south of I-86 is a quiet

full-service restaurant with good food—a good place to celebrate your paddle.

Dogs: OK
Admission: Free
Field Contributor: Laura Arney

The Genesee River from Belmont to Portageville is a fast-moving, clear water stream through a wide valley, undisturbed by human development. What is especially nice is that the inside of the many twists and turns are level gravel banks. We found it comforting to be able to scout the turns before running them and to easily portage around any turns we didn't feel confident running. Having this option makes the Genesee River a good stream to work on improving your paddling skills. The flat gravel banks also offer plenty of opportunity for breaks and picnics.

Normally by June the water level is too low to paddle. However, on a wet year, we paddled in late June and rarely scraped bottom—usually when we chose a poor line. Why is it so difficult to remember that deep water is on the outside of turns? Our instincts are to cut a more direct line across the turns, but that can result in running aground.

From Belmont to the County Road 16 bridge west of Angelica you'll find strainers at the fast-water bends. From the County Route 16 bridge north to Fillmore, you'll still find lots of ripples and even white water, but fewer strainers to worry about. Between County Road 16 and Belfast the river periodically cuts into steep banks to reveal strata that are fun for the amateur geologist to decipher. From Fillmore north to Portageville is more difficult with faster water, strainers and sharp bends. Don't continue north from Portageville or you'll tumble down the major waterfalls in Letchworth Gorge.

Paddling Directions (Belmont to Fillmore):
- From beside Phillips Creek in Belmont, head downstream under the rust colored Route 244 highway bridge.
- Van Campen Creek merges from the left.
- Pass under the green Gibson Hill Road Bridge. (The shores are posted and patrolled.)
- Paddle under the I-86 bridges.
- Paddle either channel around a big island.

- A small creek enters from the left, then Angelica Creek from the right, and you pass under power lines.
- Pass under the green, arched superstructure of County Road 16 bridge. (Downstream, right is a dirt road leading to County Road 16.)
- Paddling gets easier because the bends are now generally devoid of strainers. Enjoy the layers in the exposed banks and maybe stop for a clay bath followed by a swim.
- First White Creek, then Black Creek merges from the left.
- Pass under the green highway bridge of County Route 26 in Belfast. (Upstream, right, well before the bridge, is a dirt road leading to Hugh Street.)
- Paddle around an island.
- Pass a pillar in the river. It's all that remains of an old railroad bridge.
- Pass 5 stone gabions that reach into the water on the left. These are attempts to stabilize the bank along Route 19.
- Caneadea Creek merges from the left. It's the outflow from Rushford Lake.
- The high, rusted, silver metal bridge in Caneadea (County Route 46) is now closed to traffic. (Access is poor here.)
- Next comes the brown highway bridge of Council House Road. (Upstream, left is a muddy shore with a dirt path that turns into a road leading to Council House Road.)
- Paddle under a rusted, metal bridge that is closed to traffic. (Rocks below the bridge, right, lead to a dirt path up to the bridge near Ballard Road.)
- Pick the best route through rock ledges and boulder fields.
- Take-out is on the left, before the brown highway bridge of Route 19A (Main Street, Fillmore) where a gravel road comes down to water level.

  Note: You can continue to paddle to Portageville, but the going is more difficult. See the listings above for take-out options. Do not continue past the arched cement bridge of Route 436 in Portageville.

Date visited:

Notes:

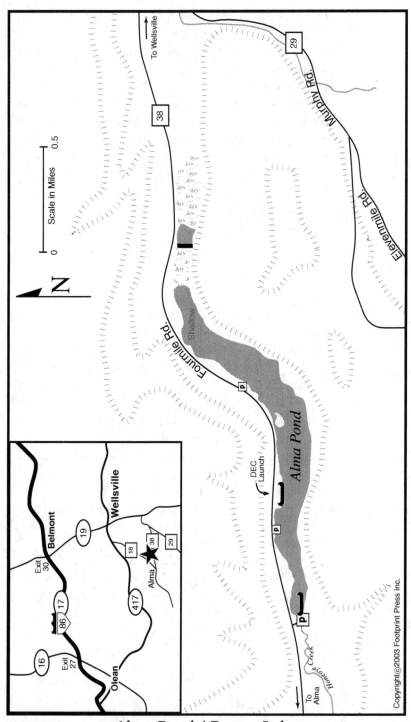

Alma Pond / Beaver Lake

19

ALMA POND / BEAVER LAKE

Location: County Road 38 (Fourmile Road), Alma, Allegany County

Directions: From Route 19 south of Wellsville, turn right onto County Road 29 South at York Corners. Turn right onto County Road 38 (Fourmile Road). The DEC parking area and launch site is 2.7 miles from this corner, on the left, marked with a sign "Alma Pond Fishing Access Site."

Launch Site #1: The DEC launch site 2.7 miles from the corner of Routes 38 and 29 has room to park 10 cars. It has a small dirt ramp with a 15-yard carry from the parking area.

Launch Site #2: 3.3 miles west of the corner of Routes 38 and 29 is a short dirt road to a parking area and launch at the dike.

Launch Sites #3&4: You can also launch from the 2 small parking areas shown on the map.

Best Season to Visit: Spring, summer and fall

Nearby Campgrounds: Evergreen Trails Campground, Allegany County Road 15, Angelica, NY 14709 (585) 466-7993, www.evergreentrails.com

Paddling Distance: The lake is 1.7 miles long. From the DEC launch site to the dike at the western end is 0.5 mile.

Estimated Time to Paddle: 2 hours or more

Difficulty: ▶━━◆

Other Activities: Fish

Amenities: None

Dogs: OK

Admission: Free

Contact: DEC, Region 9
5425 County Route 48, Belmont, NY 14813
(585) 268-5392
www.dec.state.ny.us

Watch for the resident bald eagle and osprey as you paddle this undeveloped lake with two names. It's part of Honeoye Creek, created by a dike at the western end. The eastern end has a lily swamp, marsh areas, and an island to paddle around. You'll see a few small camps around this lake. Otherwise it's all natural, a lowland nestled at the base of steep hills.

Each year the private lands on these hills are opened for the Ridgewalk and Run, the ultimate autumn outdoors event in Western New York (www.ridgewalk.com).

Paddling Directions:
  • Explore at will.

Date visited:

Notes:

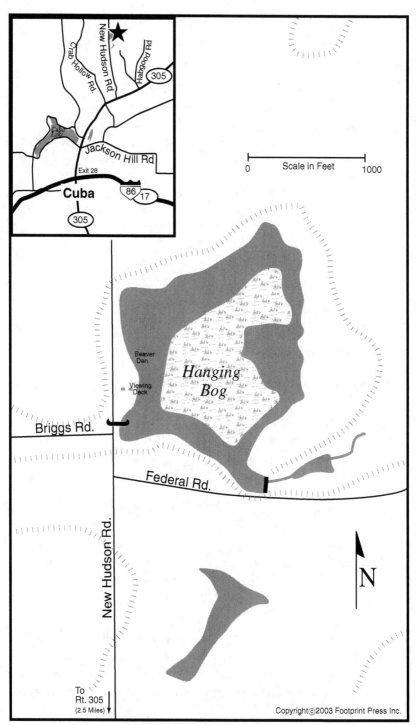

Hanging Bog Pond

20

HANGING BOG POND

Location: New Hudson, Allegany County

Directions: From I-86 (old Route 17) take exit 28 (Cuba) and head north on Route 305. Turn left (N) on New Hudson Road and head uphill. This turns into a rough, pitted dirt road. After Briggs Road on the left, watch for the unmarked DEC parking area to the right. (Caution: If you try to reach Hanging Bog from the north, expect extremely rough dirt roads.)

Launch Site #1: The dirt DEC parking area has room for ~6 cars and close access to the water. A wooden beam edges part of the launch area providing deeper water for easy launching. A path connects it to another parking area with a viewing deck.

Best Season to Visit: Summer (expect soft muddy road access in spring and hunters in fall)

Nearby Campgrounds: Write to DEC (address below) for a permit to camp in Hanging Bog Game Management Area.

Paddling Distance: Paddling around the central bog area is approximately 1.3 miles

Estimated Time to Paddle: 1 hour or more

Difficulty: ▬▬

Other Activities: Fish, hike, hunt, bird watch, find bog plants

Amenities: None

Dogs: OK

Admission: Free

Contact: DEC, Region 9
5425 County Route 48, Belmont, NY 14813
(585) 268-5392
www.dec.state.ny.us

Hanging Bog Game Management Area is a 4,500-acre state park with a 45-acre bog pond as its crown jewel. Short channels allow you to make forays into the 16-acre bog island to get a close-up view of bog plants. Hanging Bog Pond is surrounded by a pine forest and

Paddle in and out of sphagnum bogs at Hanging Bog Pond.

is home to an active colony of beavers. Look for beaver cut trees along the shore and explore their den along the western shore.

Paddling Directions:
  • Explore at will.

Date visited:

Notes:

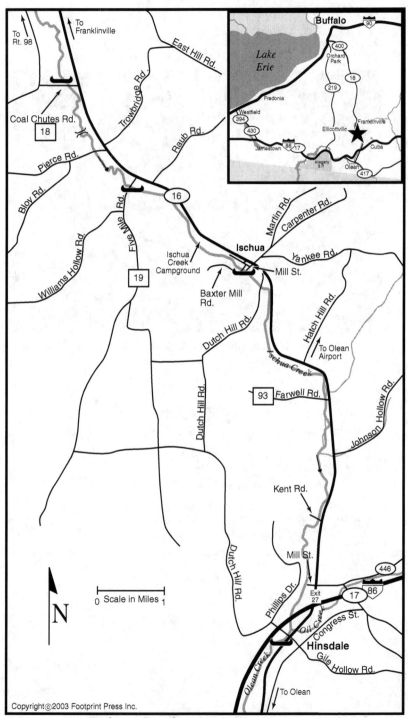

Ischua Creek (Franklinville to Hinsdale)

21

ISCHUA CREEK
(Franklinville to Hinsdale)

Location: Franklinville, Ischua and Hinsdale, Cattaraugus County

Directions: From Franklinville, head south on Route 16 for 3.5 miles. Turn right onto Coal Chutes Road and park near the bridge. Or, from I-86 take exit 27 and head north on Route 16 to Coal Chutes Road.

Launch Site #1: At Coal Chutes Road bridge carry over the guardrail and down to large rocks, upstream, right. (It is possible to start farther upstream at the Route 98 bridge over Ischua Creek (near Cadiz), 1.1 mile south of Franklinville, if the water level is high enough. Parking is along the road and river access is downstream, left.)

Launch Site #2: At Five Mile Road you can park along the road. Fishing access paths lead to water level on both the left and right, downstream shores.

Launch Site #3: In Ischua turn west on Mill Street and drive to the end, past the town DPW. Park near shore at a flat gravel bar.

Take-out Site: From Route 16 in Hinsdale turn northwest onto Gile Hollow Road. Pass over Olean Creek then just before the I-86 overpass, turn left at the "Olean Creek Fishing Access Site" sign. Follow the gravel road for 1.8 miles to the end. A grass path leads 20 yards to a mud bank that is hard to find from the water. Consider tying a colorful bandanna to a branch that's visible from the creek.

Best Season to Visit: Late spring, early summer or after a good rain

Nearby Campgrounds: Ischua Creek Campground, 5787 Route 16, Ischua, NY 14743, (716) 557-2053 tddarn@localnet.net

Valley View Campgrounds, Route 16, Ischua, NY 14746, (716) 557-2216

Paddling Distance: 12.4 miles total

Coal Chutes Rd. to Five Mile Road: 2.5 miles

Five Mile Road to Mill St., Ischua: 2.5 miles
Mill St., Ischua to the DEC take-out: 7.4 miles

Estimated Time to Paddle: 4 hours in July

Difficulty:  (fast current, sharp turns, a few portages around downed trees)

Other Activities: Fish for brown trout

Amenities: Hinsdale Memorial Park at the entrance of the DEC take-out site has a Porta-potty, pavilion, playground and baseball fields.

Dogs: OK

Admission: Free

Contact: DEC, Region 9
182 East Union Street, Allegany, N.Y. 14706
(716) 372-0645, www.dec.state.ny.us

Watch for deer around the bends in Ischua Creek.

This creek, a favorite of locals, winds through wooded areas and farmland among hills. Route 16 parallels the stream providing many access points, but it's far enough away to maintain a remote feel on the waterway. An active railroad follows the west bank of the creek. The water flows through a stone-lined streambed making it a very pretty run. In one stretch we passed 5 deer standing in the creek.

The water in this creek moves, even in mid-July. Expect many riffles and chutes, especially around islands, interspersed between flat, deep sections. We (wimps that we are) would not be comfortable paddling here in spring conditions. In mid-July we had to drag across a few shallow spots, but it was a small price to pay. In spring some of the downed trees we drifted through would have become dangerous strainers. Gravel bars along the way offer inviting picnic spots.

Paddling Directions:
- From the arched, silver Coal Chutes bridge, head downstream.
- Cross under an old, rusted farm bridge.
- Cross under the green, metal Pierce Road bridge. (Access is downstream, both left and right.)
- Cross under the Five Mile Road (County Route 19) Road bridge. (Access is downstream, both left and right.)
- Pass the campground.
- Cross under the tall, brown superstructure of Baxter Mill Road bridge.
- Shortly, downstream, left will be a gravel bank that offers easy access from the end of Mill Street, Ischua.
- Cross under the cement and silver-railed Dutch Hill Road bridge. (Marginal access is at large rocks downstream, right. A gravel road snakes back to shore from Dutch Hill Road near the railroad tracks.)
- Watch for some stonework, reported to date back 200 years to an old canal that was never completed, and some power lines.
- Cross under the silver Farwell Road bridge.
- Cross under the green, metal Kent Road bridge.
- Twist through cow pasture lands at eye level.

- Pass stone abutments and pilings in the water from a former Mill Street bridge.
- Cross under two big highway bridges for I-86.
- Oil Creek merges from the left making the waterway deeper and wider. It's now called Olean Creek. (Caution, do not put in upstream and attempt to paddle down Oil Creek. It's blocked by massive logjams.)
- Pass under the green Gile Hollow Road bridge.
- The take-out point is hard to spot from the water. After the Gile Hollow Road bridge, round a bend and pass a small island. When you see cars zip by directly ahead on I-86, watch to the right for a small mud bank.

Date visited:

Notes:

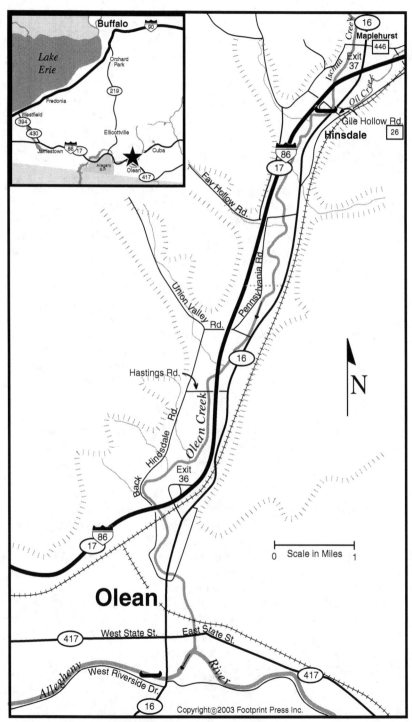

Olean Creek (Hinsdale to Olean)

22

OLEAN CREEK
(Hinsdale to Olean)

Location: North of Olean, Cattaraugus County

Directions: From I-86 (old Route 17) take exit 37 (Hinsdale) and head south on Route 16 towards Hinsdale. Turn right onto County Road 26 (Gile Hollow Road) and cross Olean Creek. On your left, before the I-86 underpass is a dirt road labeled as a DEC Fishing Access Site. Turn left and park at the end of the dirt road.

Recommended Launch Site: From the DEC Fishing Access site at County Route 26 (Gile Hollow Road) follow a grassy trail 50 yards to water's edge. There is a steep bank to a mud flat for launching.

Upstream Launch Site: You can extend your paddle 1/2 hour by launching upstream in Oil Creek. From I-86 (old Route 17) take exit 37 (Hinsdale) and head north on Route 16. Take the first right in Maplehurst onto County Road 446. Take the first right on Wagner Hill Road and cross Oil Creek. Immediately turn left on Underwood Road and park along the shoulder. Carry 50 feet down a weedy slope to launch upstream of the bridge. Oil Creek upstream of this point is not navigable. It is blocked by massive logjams.

Take-out Site: In Olean, on the Allegany River. Head south through Olean on Route 16. Cross the Allegheny River then turn right on West Riverside Drive. The first right (no sign) leads to a cement boat ramp and parking area.

Best Season to Visit: Spring, summer, fall

Paddling Distance: 9 miles from Gile Hollow Road to West Riverside Drive (or, 6.3 miles from Gile Hollow Road to Back Hinsdale Road)

Estimated Time to Paddle: 3 to 4 hours

Difficulty: (some downed trees and small chutes)

Other Activities: Fish, bird watch
Amenities: None
Dogs: OK
Admission: Free

While paddling this route at the end of July, we encountered some shallow spots but never had to get out of our kayaks. The stream was 20 to 50 feet wide with a mild current. Expect some road noise from the nearby highways, but we didn't find it intrusive. Olean Creek follows an enjoyable route through farmland and wooded areas.

Bird's eye view of a kayaker on Olean Creek.

Paddling Directions:
- From the launch point, head downstream.
- There's a big island before the first bridge. Both channels are usually open.
- Pass the cement and silver I-beams of Fay Hollow Road bridge. (Marginal access on either side of bridge to the right.)
- Pass power lines. Expect some small chutes and possible blow-downs across the creek, with narrow passages.
- The creek widens to 50-100 feet and the current slows.

- Pass Union Valley Road bridge. (Marginal access downstream, right.)
- Cross under the I-86 bridges.
- Quickly pass under the Hasting Road bridge.
- Pass some bridge abutments in the creek.
- At 6.3 miles, pass under the I-86 bridges on the outskirts of Olean. (There is an unmarked dirt parking area under the bridges on Back Hinsdale Road with room for 8 to 10 cars and easy access to the water by carrying boats over a small knoll.)
- Pass under a railroad bridge, then pass a water treatment plant on your right.
- Paddling through Olean now, you'll be in a channel with steep grassy sides. These are water control impoundments. Pass under two road bridges then a railroad bridge. If the water is shallow, you'll notice you're passing over several pipelines.
- Pass under another road bridge (E. State Street) then some old abutments before meeting the Allegheny River.
- Turn right to head downstream in the Allegheny. Paddling here in summer, we didn't notice any increase in water flow. The channel just became wider.
- Aim to the left shore as you approach the first (Route 16) bridge. The take-out is on the far side of the bridge, downstream left.

Date visited:

Notes:

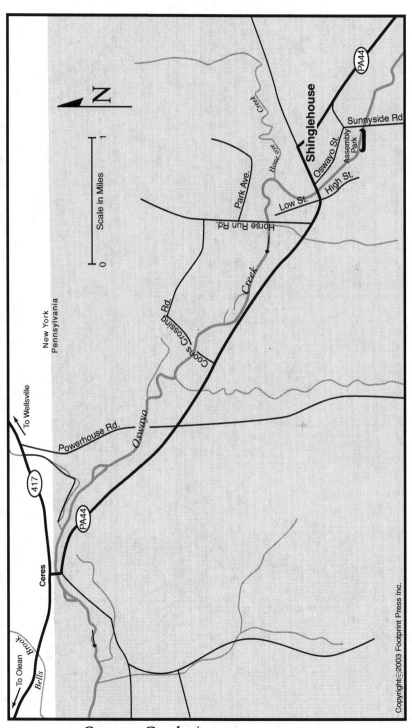

Oswayo Creek (start at Shinglehouse, PA)

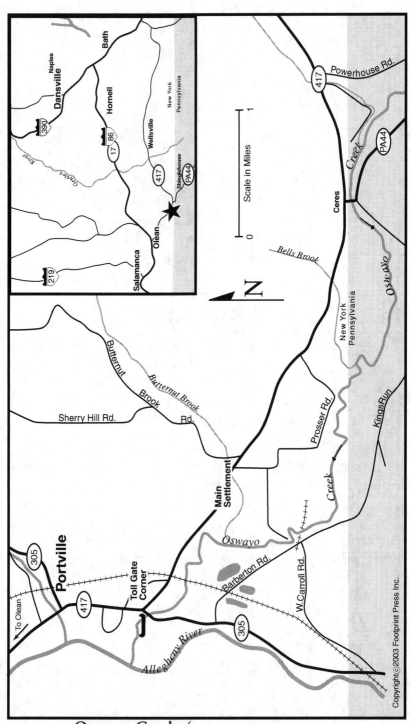

Oswayo Creek (end at Toll Gate Corner, NY)

23

OSWAYO CREEK
(Shinglehouse, PA to Toll Gate Corner, NY)

Location: Pennsylvania and Cattaraugus County, NY

Directions: From Olean head east on Route 417 or from Wellsville, head west on Route 417. At its most southern point in the town of Ceres, head southeast on PA Route 44 into Pennsylvania. In Shinglehouse, cross the Oswayo Creek then turn right onto Oswayo Street. Take another right onto Sunnyside Road. Pass the first parking lot for Assembly Park and park in the second one at the edge of Oswayo Creek.

Launch Site: Assembly Park has a 6-car lot along the creek. Follow the easy grass slope to launch downstream, right of the bridge.

Take-out Site: The Route 305 bridge at Toll Gate Corner. Park along the shoulder of Route 305 or at the entrance to the DEC flood control gate. There is a 40-yard carry across a flat grass area to the take-out point downstream, right of the bridge.

Best Season to Visit: Spring

Paddling Distance: Total: 12.4 miles (There are some emergency take out points but no good alternate launch points.)

        Sunnyside Road to PA Route 44 bridge: 6.2 miles

        PA Route 44 bridge to Toll Gate Corner: 6.2 miles

Estimated Time to Paddle: 4 to 5 hours

Difficulty:

Water Level Information: http://waterdata.usgs.gov/ny/nwis/rt (gauge #03010655 is at the start: Shinglehouse, PA)

Other Activities: Fish, bird watch, hike in Assembly Park

Amenities: None

Dogs: OK

Admission: Free

Contact: Assembly Park, Shinglehouse Borough
PO Box 156, Shinglehouse, PA 16748
(814) 697-6711

Paddling beautiful, clear Oswayo Creek near Powerhouse Road.

The name Oswayo is the English interpretation of an Indian name but no one knows for sure what it means. For most of its route, Oswayo Creek is wide (50 to 75-feet wide) and deep in springtime. There are some wide, shallow spots, which lead us to believe paddling in summer and fall may be more of a challenge. The current alternates from slow, steady to fairly fast but remains an easy paddle, with few impediments. There are plenty of islands to paddle around, but choosing a preferred route is not an issue.

What we really enjoyed on this waterway was the fact that it winds through countryside, away from any major roads and therefore was quiet and teeming with wildlife. We saw lots of deer, teal ducks, kingfishers, and followed 3 eagles downstream, getting views of these majestic birds at close range. Watch for beaver and raccoon tracks in the mud along the shores. Since you're in the wilds, there are plenty of spots that beckon for a picnic stop.

Assembly Park in Shinglehouse, PA is an active 2.5-acre community park with picnic pavilions, playgrounds, restrooms and hiking trails through the woods with covered bridges and nature identification signs. Various loops can be hiked for 0.7, 1.0 and 1.3 miles each. The Skunk Cabbage Trail is 0.3 mile long. Pets must be leashed. Don't expect any amenities on this paddle—you're heading into natural terrain.

Paddling Directions:
- From the Sunnyside Road bridge begin your downstream journey.
- Pass under Route 44 (Ceres Road) bridge.
- Pass under the Horse Run Road bridge. (Access is upstream, left. Park at a pull-off on Low Street for a sloped grassy take-out to Low Street.)
- Pass an old iron bridge that is closed to traffic at Coons Crossing Road. This is approximately the one hour mark.
- At Powerhouse Road there is a cable strung high above the creek. It's hard to see the old abutments. The bridge is gone. (Access is upstream, left, under the cable.)
- An island in the creek had both channels blocked by small downed trees when we paddled here.
- Pass under PA Route 44 after about 2 hours. This is your half way point. (No parking available here, but you can take out upstream, left, on sloped grass.)
- A long stretch with no landmarks.
- Pass abutments from an old railroad bridge.
- Pass abutments from an old road bridge. (Access is downstream, left.)
- A long stretch with no landmarks.
- Pass under an active railroad bridge.
- Pass under the Route 305 bridge and take-out downstream, right.

Date visited:

Notes:

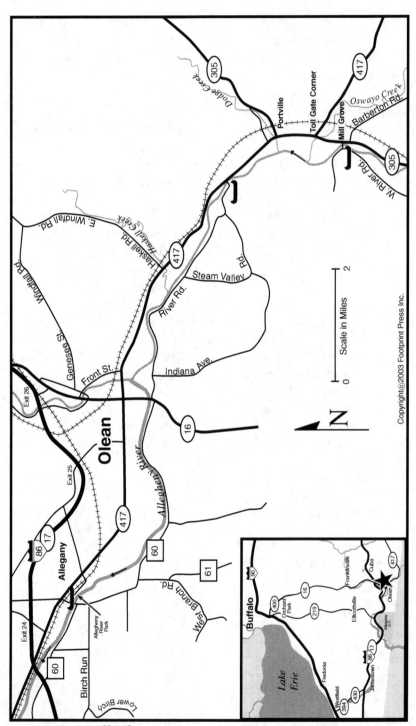

Allegheny River (Mill Grove to Portville)

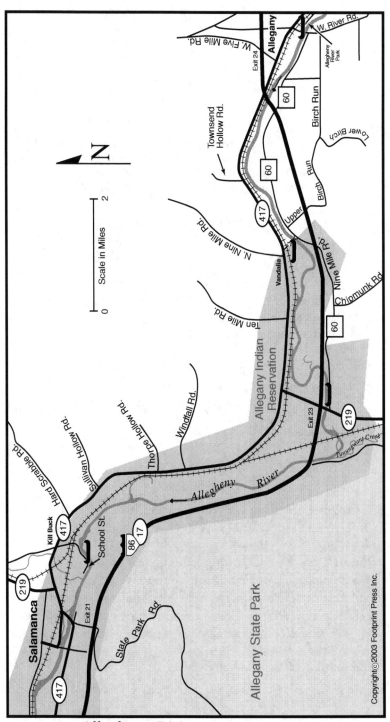

Allegheny River (Allegany to Kill Buck)

24

ALLEGHENY RIVER
(Mill Grove to Portville)

Location: Mill Grove and Portville, Cattaraugus County

Directions: From I-86 at Olean (exit 26), head south on Route 16. Turn left (E) onto Route 417. In Portville turn south on Route 305. Continue south on Route 305 through Toll Gate Corner then turn right onto West River Road. Cross the Allegheny River bridge and bear left. Park off the road, on the west side of the bridge.

Launch Site: From West River Road a grass area leads to a sand bank launch upstream, left.

Take-out Site: Upstream, left of the Steam Valley Road bridge.

Best Season to Visit: Summer

Paddling Distance: Total: 2.7 miles

Estimated Time to Paddle: 1 to 2 hours

Difficulty: ▶━■ (<2 feet per mile gradient)

Water Level Information: http://waterdata.usgs.gov/ny/nwis/uv (gauge #03011020 is on Allegheny River at Salamanca which is 28 miles below this segment)

Other Activities: Bird watch, fish for muskie

Amenities: None

Dogs: OK

Admission: Free

The Allegheny River is a wide, meandering waterway that rises in Pennsylvania, loops north through New York State then heads back down to Pennsylvania as a reservoir, with its waters backed up by the Kinzua Dam. It has a long history of human use, beginning as part of a portage route to the Mississippi River by the Native Americans and early explorers. From the early 1800s until the virgin pine and hemlock were depleted, lumber was a major product of the area. Olean was used as a collection point for rafts of lumber. Submerged posts in the river bed are evidence of old booms and dams that once controlled the flow of logs in the river.

A bridge spans the wide Allegheny River.

The first oil well was dug in the area in 1865. By the 1880s Olean had over 300 oil storage tanks, making it the largest oil storage depot in the world. Around 1927 it became cheaper to ship oil via tankers from the Middle East and Olean's oil business died.

A major flood in 1942 caused massive damage and resulted in the building of levees along the Allegheny River. In 1972 Hurricane Agnes raised water levels to within 1 foot of the top of the levees.

Today the Allegheny River is wide with a mild current (except during spring high waters) and often has high mud banks. Flood control dikes, set back from the water's edge, parallel the river, making this feel like a river within a river. You can paddle most of the Allegheny, but some sections are more scenic than others:

- Eldred, PA to Mill Grove: some ripples, submerged pilings, steep banks
- Mill Grove to Steam Valley Road in Portville (the segment described below): submerged pilings, dikes set back

- Portville, Olean, and Allegany to Vandalia: urban and industrial, two large pipes cross the river in Olean and may pose impediments in shallow water
- Vandalia to Salamanca (the section described on page 121): wild, Indian Reservation land, submerged pilings near Tunungwant Creek
- Salamanca to Red House: some riffles
- Allegheny Reservoir: irregular, wooded banks, can be rough in wind, used by motorboats

In this stretch (Mill Grove to Portville) watch for ospreys and green herons along the oak-lined banks. Flood control dikes parallel the river but are set back a bit, leaving the natural high mud and sand banks of the river as your primary view.

Paddling Directions:

- From the West River Road bridge, head downstream.
- Maneuver through your private slalom course made by wood pilings from lumbering days.
- Oswayo Creek merges from the right. (See page 113 for details on paddling this creek.)
- Dodge Creek merges from the right.
- Take-out is upstream, left at the tall, cement Steam Valley Road bridge. (You can continue downstream through the urban and industrialized sections if you wish. It's another 10 miles to Allegheny River Park in Allegany.)

Date visited:

Notes:

25

ALLEGHENY RIVER
(Allegany to Kill Buck)

Location: Allegany, Vandalia and Kill Buck, Cattaraugus County

Directions: From I-86 at Allegany (exit 24), head south on West Five Mile Road to Route 417. Turn left onto Route 417, then take the first right onto West River Road. Take the first left onto Union Street and park on the right at Allegheny River Park

Launch Site #1: Allegheny River Park on West Union Street in Allegany has a 50-yard carry across a grass field from the parking lot to the river bank.

Launch Site #2: The South Nine Mile Road bridge is closed to traffic. From Route 417 in Vandalia, turn south onto South Nine Mile Road and park before the closed bridge. A short grass bank leads to the river downstream, right.

Take-out Site #1: Upstream, left of the Route 219 bridge is a cement pier and an accessible dirt bank. From Route 219, turn east on Nine Mile Road. Continue straight when the road bends onto a dirt access road that leads to below the bridge.

Take-out Site #2: A dirt road runs into the water on the right bank in Kill Buck, where School Street parallels the river. This take-out is harder to spot from the river. From Route 417, east of Salamanca, turn south on School Street and follow it over two sets of railroad tracks until it turns into a dirt road and meets the river. The area is heavily littered with trash.

Best Season to Visit: Summer

Paddling Distance: Total: 15.8 miles

Allegheny River Park to S. Nine Mile Road: 4.4 miles
S. Nine Mile Road to Route 219: 4.6 miles
Route 219 to School Street: 6.8 miles

Estimated Time to Paddle: 5 to 6 hours

Difficulty: ▬● (<2 feet per mile gradient)

Water Level Information: http://waterdata.usgs.gov/ny/nwis/uv (gauge #03011020 is on Allegheny River at Salamanca, which is 2 miles below this segment)

Other Activities: Bird watch (fishing on the reservation requires a special permit)

Amenities: Allegheny River Park has a picnic pavilion, playground and sports fields

Dogs: OK

Admission: Free

See page 118 for a history and description of the Allegheny River. This section (Allegany to Kill Buck) is mainly through undeveloped Indian Reservation land. Watch for submerged pilings near Tunungwant Creek.

Paddling Directions:
- From Allegheny River Park, head downstream.
- The next bridge has double green arches. It's the closed South Nine Mile Road bridge and marks the beginning of the Allegany Indian Reservation. (Access is downstream, right.)
- The river sweeps around more turns.
- A cement pier and sand bank are upstream, left of the high, brown Route 219 highway bridge.
- Pass under a railroad trestle.
- Tunungwant Creek merges from the left. Be alert for vertical log piles concealed below the surface.
- Watch for the School Street take-out on the right bank.

Date visited:

Notes:

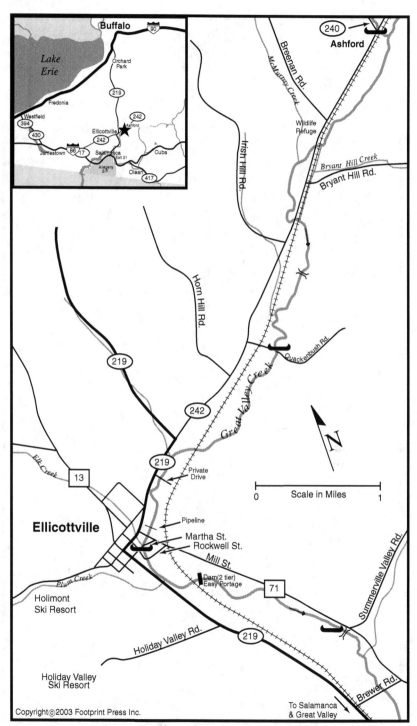

Great Valley Creek (start at Ashford)

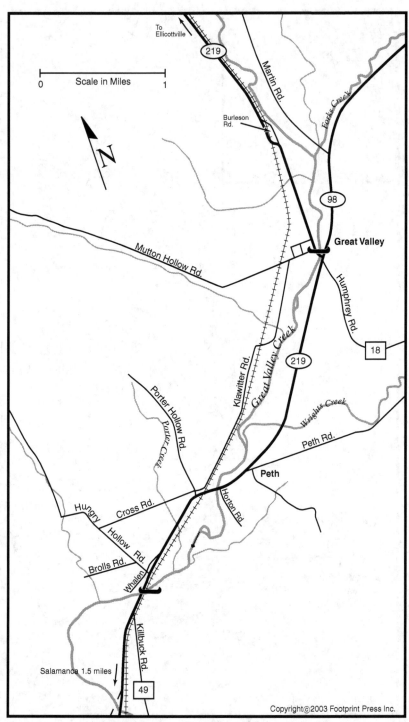

Great Valley Creek (end at Salamanca)

26

GREAT VALLEY CREEK
(Ashford to Salamanca)

Location: Ashford, Ellicottville, Great Valley and Salamanca, Cattaraugus County

Directions: From I-86 (old Route 17) take exit 21 (Salamanca) and head north on Route 219 through Ellicottville. Turn north on Route 242 to the Beaver Meadow Creek bridge in Ashford at the corner of Route 240 (West Valley Road). Park along the road.

Launch Site #1: Park off the road just south of the Route 242 bridge, but carry across the bridge and put into Beaver Meadow Creek from the north side. It's a 25-yard carry to a gradually sloped bank.

Launch Site #2: Park along Quackenbush Road and launch downstream, left via an easy bank.

Launch Site #3: Park along Martha Street in Ellicottville (the middle bridge) for easy access downstream, left.

Launch Site #4: Park near a farm bridge at the tractor path across from Summerville Valley Road. Do not block the bridge. Stream access is via a gradual tractor path upstream, left.

Launch Site #5: Park at Karlie's Restaurant and Hot Dog Stand on Route 219 next to the creek in Great Valley. Follow a path toward the bridge that leads to a grass bank launch upstream, right.

Take-out Site: 1.5 miles north of Salamanca, from Route 219 turn west onto Hungry Hollow Road, then quickly left onto Whalen Road. Turn left into a tractor trailer parking area and drive across the grass field to the creek edge. Launch is via the grass bank downstream, right.

Best Season to Visit: Spring (need medium to high water)

Nearby Campgrounds: Red House Area Campground, on ASP1 in Allegany State Park is 5 miles south of Salamanca. Call 1-800-456-CAMP for reservations. (Cabins are also available for rent in the Red House area.)

Paddling Distance: Total: 15.9 miles

Ashford to Quackenbush Road: 3.6 miles (1.5 hrs.)
Quackenbush Road to Martha St.: 2.3 miles (1 hr.)
Martha Street to tractor path: 2.4 miles (0.75 hr.)
Tractor path to Great Valley: 3.8 miles (1.75 hrs.)
Great Valley to Whalen Road: 3.8 miles (1 hr.)

Estimated Time to Paddle: 5 to 6 hours in spring

Difficulty: (sharp bends, one low dam downstream of Ellicottville, 15 feet per mile gradient)

Other Activities: Fish for brown and rainbow trout

Amenities: The Store and Restaurant is at launch site #1

Dogs: OK

Admission: Free

Just south of Ashford, Beaver Meadow Creek and Devereaux Branch merge to form Great Valley Creek. The 15 feet per mile gradient is fairly consistent throughout the 13 miles, so this is moving water with riffles but no white-water. It has to be run in medium to high water and is a great novice to intermediate run. Even in spring, we poled through many stretches in the upper reaches. However, north of Ellicottville is wild and scenic with lots of wildlife, so it's worth the extra effort. We paddled next to baby beavers, passed Canada geese guarding their nests, flocks of Merganser ducks and lots of song birds and woodchucks on this stretch in April. If poling isn't your thing, begin at Quackenbush Road or, better yet, in Ellicottville. From Quackenbush Road to Ellicottville there are some mild chutes and trees to maneuver around.

South of Ellicottville the creek is deeper and easier but less scenic. You're in a wide farm valley often with a suburban feel. Sporadically chunks of cement slabs line the banks.

You could continue past the take-out to the Allegheny River but it's not recommended. The semi-urban scenery is unappealing. There's a great take-out downstream, right of the Route 417 bridge where a dirt road runs down to water level.

Paddling Directions:
- From the Route 242 bridge in Ashford, head downstream.
- Turn right to continue downstream in Great Valley Creek.
- Pass through a wildlife refuge area.

A pleasant paddle on Great Valley Creek.

- Cross under a railroad bridge then quickly another Route 242 bridge.
- Reverse this order with a Route 242 bridge followed quickly by a railroad bridge.
- Pass under a small wooden bridge. Portage around a downed tree. The stream is still quite shallow.
- Pass under the low, silver-railed Quackenbush Road bridge (access downstream, left).
- Run through some minor chutes.
- After a long, winding stretch, pass under another railroad bridge.
- Pass under a private, red-metal farm bridge as you approach the outskirts of Ellicottville.
- A pipeline will run overhead, then the first of three bridges (Mill Street, Martha Street and Rockwell Street) in quick

succession in Ellicottville. (Martha Street has good access downstream, left.)

- Great Valley Creek bends to head south. Plum Creek merges from the right and you pass bridge abutments.
- Pass under a railroad bridge followed quickly by a low dam with two tiers. Pull-out to the right for an easy portage around the dam.
- The creek will approach Mill Street (County Route 71) to the right. (There is road-side parking and good stream access.)
- Pass under the an old farm bridge. (A tractor path downstream, left provides good access.)
- Pass under the Brewer Road bridge. (Park along the road and access the stream from the right.)
- The creek is in a wide, steep-sided valley, but proceeds with a few meanders.
- Bear right as Forks Creek merges from the left.
- Pass under the brown Route 219 bridge in Great Valley. (Access is upstream, right at a grass bank.)
- Wright's Creek merges from the left.
- Pass under a Route 219 bridge.
- Paddle around some big islands.
- Just after a railroad bridge is the final Route 219 bridge and the take-out point, downstream, right. (If you continue downstream through Salamanca, there's a great take-out downstream, right of the Route 417 bridge, where a dirt road runs down to water level.)

Date visited:

Notes:

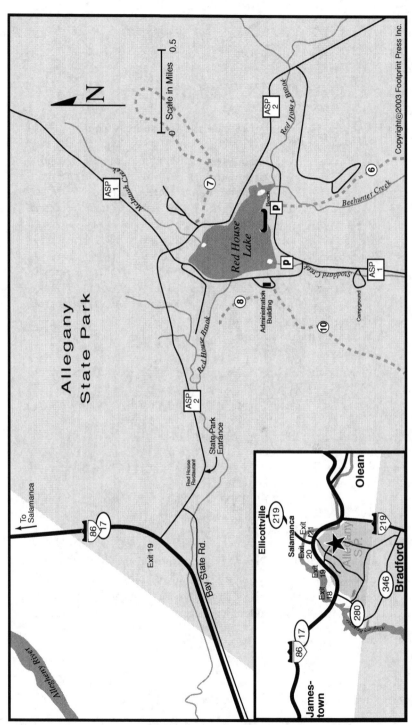

Red House Lake

27

RED HOUSE LAKE

Location: Allegany State Park, Cattaraugus County
Directions: From I-86 (old Route 17) take exit 19 (Allegany
                      State Park, Red House) and follow the signs into
                      Allegany State Park, on ASP2. Pass the entrance
                      gate. Turn right onto ASP1. Pass the administrative
                      building. At the "T" turn left then take the second
                      left into the Red House Lake beach parking area.
Launch & Take-out Site: Launch from the beach
Best Season to Visit: Spring, summer and fall
Nearby Campgrounds: Red House Area Campground, on ASP1.
                      Call 1-800-456-CAMP for reservations. (Cabins
                      are also available for rent in the Red House area.)
Paddling Distance: Red House Lake is 0.7 mile long
Estimated Time to Paddle: 1 hour or more
Difficulty: ▶━━━

Other Activities: Hike (Allegany State Park is loaded with hiking
                      trails), bike (Red House Area has a paved bike
                      trail), swim at the sandy beach, rent a boat, fish,
                      play tennis
Amenities: Picnic tables, bath house
Dogs: OK
Admission: Free Mon. - Fri., $6 entrance fee Sat. & Sun.
Contact: Allegany State Park
                      2373 ASP Route 1, Suite 3, Salamanca, NY 14779
                      (716) 354-9101
                      www.nyparks.com

Bring your fishing pole and angle for brown and rainbow trout on
this placid lake, or just paddle around to enjoy the marshy edges,
lilies and clear water. Red House Area is a great family camping
destination that offers enough variety to keep the whole family busy.

Date visited:

Notes:

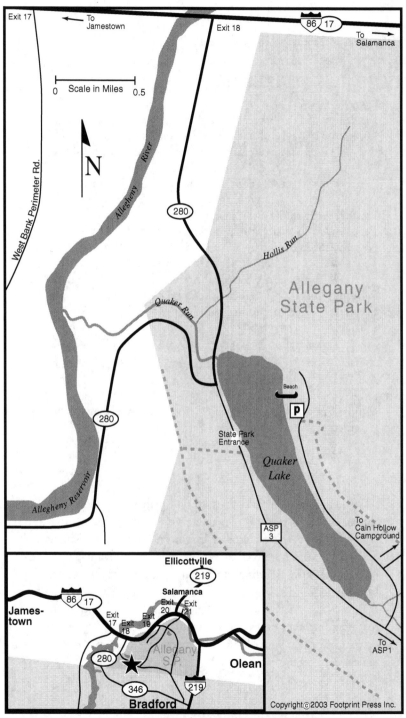

Quaker Lake

28

QUAKER LAKE

Location: Allegany State Park, Cattaraugus County
Directions: From I-86 (old Route 17) take exit 18 and head south on Route 280. Continue into Allegany State Park on ASP3. Pass the entrance gate then take the first left to find the Quaker Lake beach area parking.
Launch & Take-out Site: Launch from the beach
Best Season to Visit: Spring, summer and fall
Nearby Campgrounds: Cain Hollow Campground, off ASP3. Call 1-800-456-CAMP for reservations. (Cabins are also available for rent in the Quaker Lake area.)
Paddling Distance: Quaker Lake is 1.7 miles long
Estimated Time to Paddle: 1 hour or more
Difficulty: ▶━━━
Other Activities: Hike (Allegany State Park is loaded with hiking trails), swim at the sandy beach, rent a boat, fish
Amenities: Picnic tables, bath house
Dogs: OK
Admission: Free Mon. - Fri., $6 entrance fee Sat. & Sun.
Contact: Allegany State Park
2373 ASP Route 1, Suite 3, Salamanca, NY 14779
(716) 354-9101
www.nyparks.com

Quaker Lake is created by a dam on Quaker Run. Its outflow joins the Allegheny Reservoir. This reservoir was created in the 1960s when the U.S. Army Corps of Engineers constructed Kinzua Dam across the Allegheny River in Warren, Pennsylvania, as a flood control measure. Building the Kinzua Dam was highly controversial because it flooded one-third of the Allegany Reservation of the Seneca Nation of Indians. Nearly six hundred Senecas were forced to abandon their homes and relocate, despite a 1794 treaty that had guaranteed them those lands in perpetuity. Today the reservoir is a haven for recreation.

Quaker Lake is a quiet place for a leisurely paddle. Have you noticed the various spellings of Allegany/Allegheny? It's spelled Allegheny in Pennsylvania, and since the reservoir is mostly in Pennsylvania, its name is Allegheny Reservoir. New York entrenched the Allegany spelling into law when it created Allegany State Park.

Kayaks line the beach at Quaker Lake.

Paddling Directions:
  • Explore at will.

Date visited:

Notes:

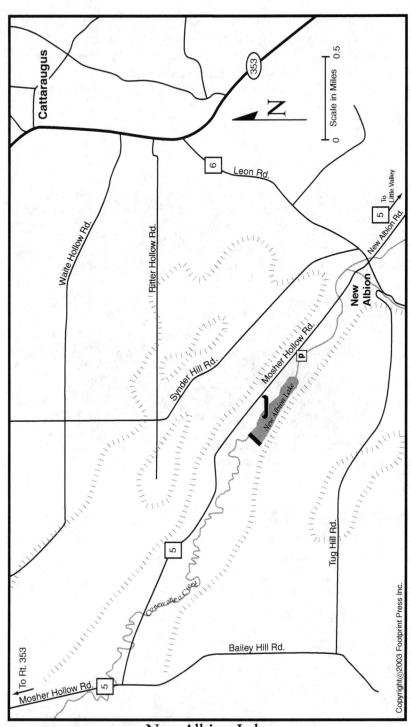

New Albion Lake

29

NEW ALBION LAKE

Location: New Albion, Cattaraugus County

Directions: From the south, take Route 353 north out of Salamanca then County Route 5 (New Albion Road) north from Little Valley. From the north, take Route 62 from Buffalo, through Gowanda. South of Gowanda, turn south on Route 353, then south on County Route 5 (Mosher Hollow Road). The DEC parking area and launch site is on the south side of County Route 5 (Mosher Hollow Road) at New Albion Lake, marked with a sign "New Albion Lake Fishing Access Site."

Launch and Take-out Site: The DEC launch site has a 30-car parking area with a short carry to a sloped gravel hand launch.

Best Season to Visit: Spring, summer and fall

Paddling Distance: The lake is 0.5 mile long

Estimated Time to Paddle: 0.5 hour or more

Difficulty: ▬▬

Other Activities: Fish (trout, bass, crappie) (Swimming, camping and picnicking are not allowed.)

Amenities: Porta-potty near the parking area

Dogs: OK

Admission: Free

Contact: DEC, Region 9
5425 County Route 48, Belmont, NY 14813
(585) 268-5392
www.dec.state.ny.us

New Albion Lake was created in 1984 when a 39-foot earthen dam was constructed along Conewango Creek near the hamlet of New Albion. The dam created a 50-acre, long, narrow pool that is 16 feet deep. It is stocked with fish, especially brown and rainbow trout, which makes this lake a prime fishing spot. Nestled against a treed hillside on the southwest bank, this lake is pristine and quiet.

Paddling Directions:
- Explore at will.

Date visited:

Notes:

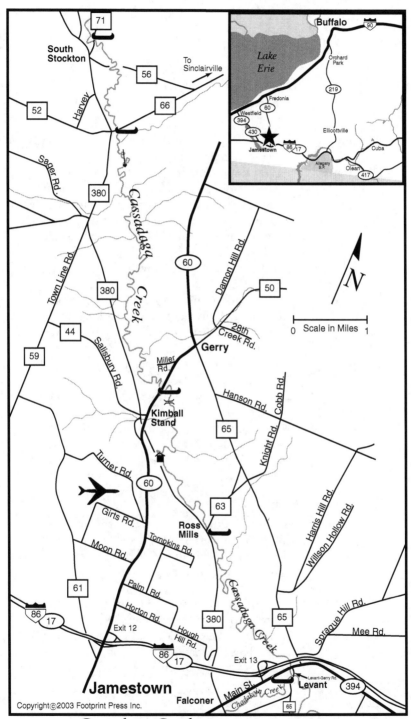

Cassadaga Creek (South Stockton to Levant)

30

CASSADAGA CREEK
(South Stockton to Levant)

Location: South Stockton, Kimball Stand, Ross Mills and Levant, Chautauqua County

Directions: From I-86 in Jamestown head north (exit 12) on Route 60 for 3.1 miles. Turn left onto County Route 44 then a quick right onto County Route 380. Follow Route 380 north then turn right onto County Route 71. Take 71 north for 100 yards and look for the rust-red "South Stockton - Marden E. Cobb Waterway Trail" sign before the bridge.

Launch Site #1:   A 6-car parking area off Route 71. There's a small wooden ramp 50-feet from the parking lot.

Launch Site #2:   A 10-car parking area is off County Route 66 (near the junction with County Route 380), on the east side of the creek, marked by a rust-red "Red Bird - Marden E. Cobb Waterway Trail" sign. A 100-foot mowed-grass path leads to the step-type launch upstream of the bridge.

Launch Site #3:   Northeast of the Route 60 bridge, at the end of the guardrail, look for a gravel road before white house #4143. It leads to the Gerry Fire Department's dry hydrant (orange posts). You can drive almost to creekside, where access is down a grass and mud bank.

Launch Site #4:   An 8-car parking area is at the corner of Routes 380 & 63 in Ross Mills, marked by a rust-red "Ross Mills - Marden E. Cobb Waterway Trail" sign. A steep bank leads to water level, downstream, left.

Take-out Site: From Route 394 east of Falconer, turn south on Route 65 (Levant-Gerry Road) and left at the brown sign "Levant - Marden E. Cobb Waterway Trail." This old road has room for 15 cars and steps down to a platform on Cassadaga Creek.

Continuing Downstream: The Cassadaga continues another 8.3 miles past the Levant take-out until it joins Conewango Creek. You can continue paddling 11.8 miles from Levant, down the Cassadaga and Conewango to take-out at Frewsburg. See details on Conewango Creek on page 146.

Best Season to Visit: Late spring or early summer

Nearby Campgrounds: A lean-to is available along the creek, 2 miles south of the Route 60 bridge. (Car access is from Route 380. An unmarked path leads from the end of a guardrail.)

Woodside Campground, Griswald Road, Cassadaga, NY 14718, (716) 672-4402

Top-A-Rise Campground, RD1 Dean School Road, Falconer, NY 14733, (716) 287-3222

Paddling Distance: Total: 19.9 miles (Route 71 to Route 65)
Route 71 to Route 66: 3.0 miles (1.5 hours)
Route 66 to Route 60: 7.9 miles (3 hours)
Route 60 to the lean-to: 2 miles (1 hour)
Route 60 to Route 63: 4.0 miles (2 hours)
Route 63 to Route 65 (take-out): 5.0 miles (2 hrs.)
Route 65 to Conewango Creek: 8.3 miles
Route 65 to Conewango Creek lean-to: 18.5 miles

Estimated Time to Paddle: 8 to 9 hours in summer

Difficulty: (slow, steady current, potential downed trees)

Other Activities: Fish for muskellunge, bass and panfish

Amenities: A privy and picnic table at the lean-to south of the Route 60 bridge.
The take-out has picnic tables and an authentic 1883 iron railroad bridge on display.

Dogs: OK

Admission: Free

Field Contributors: Ray & Carolyn Shea

Contact: Chautauqua County Dept. of Parks and Recreation 2105 South Maple Avenue, Ashville, NY 14710 (716) 763-8928

Chautauqua County Parks has developed Cassadaga Creek and Conewango Creek, two excellent flat-water waterways, into the Marden E. Cobb Waterway Trail by providing parking areas and launch sites near bridges and even supplying camping shelters along

A lean-to for camping along Cassadaga Creek.

the route. Without their dedicated maintenance this waterway would quickly become clogged with downed trees and logjams. A detailed brochure is available from Chautauqua County Parks.

This is a quiet, rural paddle with little shoreline development. Unlike so many other waterways, there's no expressway paralleling this creek. You'll feel like Lewis & Clark exploring the wilds of America. The channel is narrow and at times bushes overhanging from the shores reach to brush your shoulders. Then it widens to 20 or 30-feet. It never stops winding. In high water you should find some quiet little backwaters to explore. Wildlife is abundant. Watch for turkeys, muskrats, beavers, deer, snakes, turtles, kingfishers, kingbirds, red tailed hawks, swans and goldfinches that all call this waterway home. Blowdowns occur regularly and the beavers are industrious. It takes time to get blockages cleared away, so always be on the lookout for trees and beaver dams across this meandering creek. We paddled it in late July and found muddy water with minimal current, but we never had to push due to low water.

Paddling Directions:

- From the County Route 71 launch, head downstream.
- Cross under the closed, low, yellow-railed County Road 56 bridge.
- In 3 miles cross under the green, metal County Road 66 bridge. (A step-type launch and parking area is upstream, left.)
- Two steel pillars with wood between them are all that remain of the old Miller Road bridge.
- 200 yards before the silver-railed Route 60 bridge is a muddy bank pull-out on the left. It's hard to see from the water. This is launch site #3, the Gerry Fire Department's dry hydrant.
- Paddle under the Route 60 bridge. You've come 8 miles.
- A half mile past Route 60, a wooden snowmobile bridge spans Cassadaga Creek. Depending on water level, you may need to portage around it.
- Two miles downstream from Route 60, watch to the right (W) for a lean-to. A privy is available here.
- Cross under the rusted silver Ross Mills bridge. (There's access downstream, left via a steep bank to a parking lot at the corner of Routes 380 & 63.)
- Pass under the double bridges of I-86 and then the Route 394 bridge.
- The Chadakoin River merges from the right. Take-out immediately after the confluence at the stairway on the right. It leads to a large parking area. (If you continue downstream, it's 11.7 miles to the next take-out at Frewsburg, see page 146.)

Date visited:

Notes:

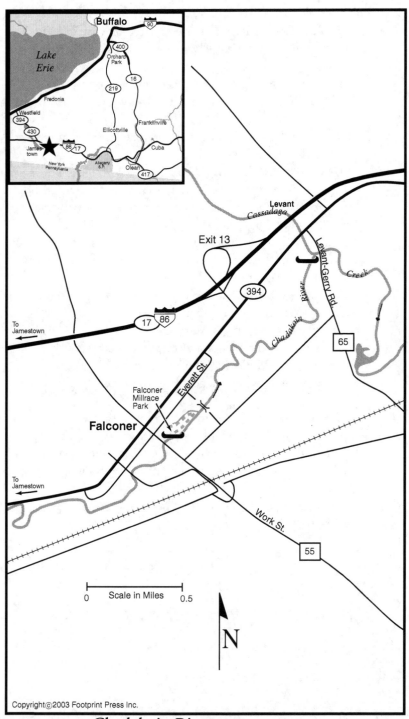

Chadakoin River (Falconer to Levant)

31

CHADAKOIN RIVER
(Falconer to Levant)

Location: Falconer, Chautauqua County

Directions: From I-86 at Falconer (exit 13), head south on Route 394. At the first light, turn left onto Work Street, then take the first left onto Everett Street. Turn right into the parking lot of the Fancher Chair Factory and drive to the back corner, into Falconer Millrace Park.

Launch Site #1:   Falconer Millrace Park has a 15-car parking lot and a floating dock.

Take-out Site: From Route 394 east of Falconer, turn south on Route 65 (Levant-Gerry Road) and left at the brown sign "Levant - Marden E. Cobb Waterway Trail." This old road has room for 15 cars and steps down to a platform on Cassadaga Creek.

Continuing Downstream: Cassadaga Creek continues downstream for 8.3 miles (see page 139) until it meets the Conewango Creek (see page 146). You can continue paddling down Conewango Creek for 11.8 miles to the Pennsylvania border.

Best Season to Visit: Spring or early summer

Paddling Distance: Total: 1.8 miles

Estimated Time to Paddle: 30 minutes

Difficulty: (fast current in spring, one narrow chute and a sharp 90 degree turn, downed trees to maneuver around)

Water Level Information: http://waterdata.usgs.gov/ny/nwis/uv (gauge #03014500 is on Chadakoin River at Falconer)

Other Activities: Hike (Falconer Park has a small nature trail)

Amenities: Falconer Millrace Park has picnic tables. The take-out has picnic tables and an authentic 1883 iron railroad bridge on display.

Dogs: OK

Admission: Free

Contact: Chautauqua County Dept. of Parks and Recreation
2105 South Maple Avenue, Ashville, NY 14710
(716) 763-8928

The water flow in this stretch of river is highly affected by rainfall and controlled by an upstream dam. We found the flow to be a bit much for novices at over 700 cubic feet per second on a spring day. By watching the on-line gage, within a few days it was down to about 500 cubic feet per second, a much more manageable rate. Be sure to check the on-line water gage before heading out. At low water this stream is unnavigable.

However, with the right level of water, this can be a fun stream. It begins on a straight section with a low pedestrian bridge then adds the excitement of a chute, a sharp turn and trees to dodge. The lower half is wide and flat. When the Chadakoin merges with the Cassadaga, you bear right for the take-out.

Falconer Millrace Park's complete name is Abe Mattison Millrace Park. It was created in 2000 and named after the village's longtime mayor. The millrace was an artificial waterway diverted from the Chadakoin River that was used to float timber to the region's furniture manufacturers. By following the small loop nature trail you can walk beside the old millrace.

Paddling Directions:
- From Falconer Millrace Park, head downstream.
- Pass under a low pedestrian bridge in 300 yards.
- Be prepared for a small chute and a sharp bend.
- When you meet the confluence of the slower moving Cassadaga Creek, turn right, downstream and head to the right bank for the take-out platform before the Route 65 bridge.

Date visited:

Notes:

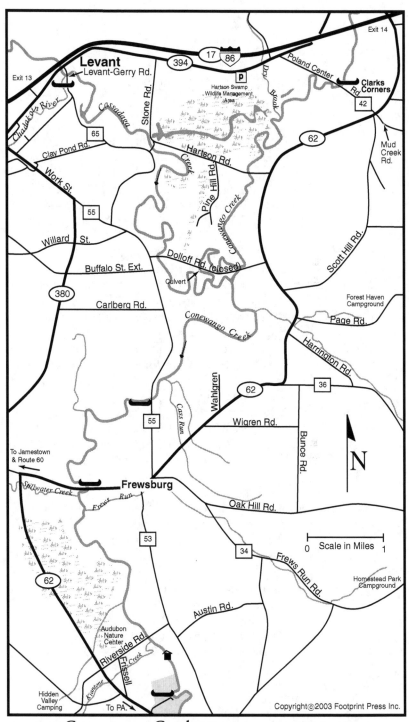

Conewango Creek (Clarks Corners to Frewsburg)

32

~~~~~

CONEWANGO CREEK
(Clarks Corners to Frewsburg)

Location: Clarks Corners/Poland Center and Frewsburg, Chautauqua County

Directions: From I-86 take exit 14 and head south on Route 62. Turn right on County Route 42 (Poland Center Road) to the Conewango Creek parking area marked by the rust-red sign "Clarks Corners - Marden E. Cobb Waterway Trail."

Launch Site #1: A 4-car parking area off County Route 42 has a stairway launch upstream of the bridge.

Launch Site #2: A 4-car parking area is off Route 55 in Frewsburg marked by the rust-red sign "Marden E. Cobb Waterway Trail." Water access is a sloped wooden ramp downstream, left.

Launch Site #3: A 4-car parking area with a gently sloping grass bank launch on the northeast side of the Route 62 bridge marked by the rust-red sign "Marden E. Cobb Waterway Trail."

Take-out Site: A 10-car parking area off Route 62, south of Frewsburg marked by the rust-red sign "Marden E. Cobb Waterway Trail." It's across from the blue "Welcome to Pennsylvania" sign. Drive to the far end of the gravel road to find a multi-level wooden dock.

Continuing Downstream: The Conewango enters Pennsylvania below this point. Canoes and kayaks must be registered in PA to use the state-maintained launch facilities.

Best Season to Visit: Summer or fall

Nearby Campgrounds: Two lean-to's are available on a county-owned island with a dock in Conewango Creek, 1 mile south of the Riverside Road bridge. Forest Haven Campground, 2329 Page Road, Kennedy, NY 14747-9717, (716) 267-5902

Hidden Valley Camping Area, 299 Kiantone
Road, Jamestown, NY 14701, (716) 569-5433
www.hiddenvalleycampingarea.com
Homestead Park Campground, PO Box 69, Frews
Run Road, Frewsburg, NY 14738
(716) 569-4666

Paddling Distance: Total: 19.3 miles
County Route 42 to County Route 55: 11 miles
County Route 55 to Route 62: 2.7 miles
Route 62 to Route 62 south of Frewsburg: 5.6 miles

Estimated Time to Paddle: 7 to 8 hours in summer

Difficulty: (slow, steady current, easy riffles, potential downed trees and beaver dams)

Water Level Information: http://pa.waterdata.usgs.gov/nwis/rt
(gauge #03015000 is on Conewango Creek at
Russell, PA, south of this segment)

Other Activities: Fish for muskellunge

Amenities: Privy at the lean-to on the island
Picnic table at the Route 62 take-out

Dogs: OK

Admission: Free

Contact: Chautauqua County Dept. of Parks and Recreation
2105 South Maple Avenue, Ashville, NY 14710
(716) 763-8928

Chautauqua County Parks has developed Cassadaga Creek and
Conewango Creek, two excellent flat-water waterways, into the
Marden E. Cobb Waterway Trail by providing parking areas and
launch sites near bridges and even supplying camping shelters along
the route. Without their diligent maintenance these waterways
would clog with blowdowns and logjams. A detailed brochure is
available from Chautauqua County Parks. See the information on
Cassadaga Creek on page 139.

Conewango Creek is a slow, meandering, muddy waterway with
many overhanging trees. Initially, the banks are steep and it's common
to see freshly uprooted trees. You may have to portage over downed
trees and beaver dams. A highlight is the county-owned island,
complete with two lean-to's south of Frewsburg. River otter have
been reintroduced to this stream, so keep an eye out for them.

Upstream from this section, the water is sluggish through marshes and straight through a long state drainage ditch, not particularly appealing. Downstream the Conewango flows into Pennsylvania and meets the Allegheny River at Warren, Pennsylvania.

Paddling Directions:
- From the County Route 42 bridge head downstream, under the rusted silver bridge.
- Dry Brook merges from the right.
- Paddle under the rusted Hartson Road highway bridge.
- Cassadaga Creek merges from the right in a profusion of channels and islands. Bear left to paddle under the closed Dolloff Road bridge.
- The creek is now wider and more river-like.
- Pass the cement pillar from an old railroad trestle, followed quickly by the Route 55 bridge at the north end of Frewsburg. (Access to a parking area is downstream, left of the bridge.)
- Cross under the grey Route 62 highway bridge west of Frewsburg. (A sloping grass bank upstream, left leads to a parking area.)
- Pass under the silver-railed Riverside Road highway bridge.
- Stillwater Creek and Frews Run merge from the right and left, respectively.
- 1.1 mile from Riverside Road bridge, you'll pass the island with lean-to's and privys.
- A half mile past the island is the take-out point. Watch for a multi-level wooden dock to the right.

Date visited:

Notes:

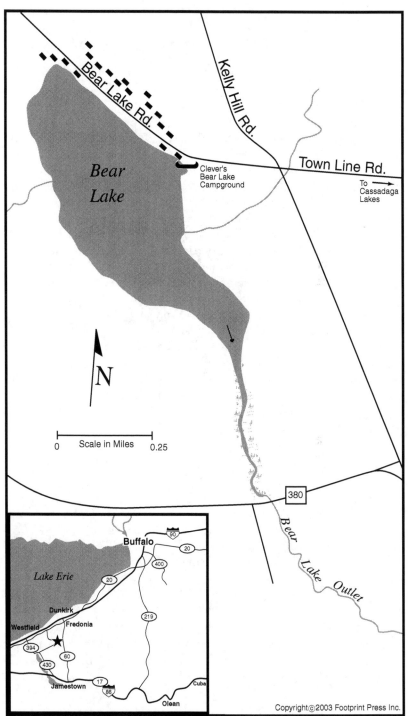

Bear Lake

Copyright©2003 Footprint Press Inc.

33

BEAR LAKE

Location: Stockton, Chautauqua County
Directions: From the New York State Thruway (I-90) take exit 59 at Dunkirk and Fredonia. Head south on Route 60, then west on Route 20 into Fredonia. In Fredonia, turn left (S) on Chautauqua Road. Take another left (S) onto Bear Lake Road and watch for the launch site to your right marked by the DEC sign "Bear Lake Fishing Access Site."
Launch Site #1: A sloped grassy bank at the 5-car parking area. (Directly behind the free grassy bank is the paved launch ramp of Clever's Bear Lake Campground. It costs $3 to use this ramp.)
Best Season to Visit: Spring, summer and fall
Nearby Campgrounds: Clever's Bear Lake Campground
8039 Bear Lake Road, Stockton, NY 14622
(716) 792-9754
Paddling Distance: Launch to County Road 380: 1.0 mile
Paddle around Bear Lake: 2.0 miles
Estimated Time to Paddle: 1 hour or more
Difficulty: ⊢━━●
Other Activities: Boat rentals available
Amenities: Picnic table at the launch
Dogs: OK
Admission: Free
Contact: DEC, Region 9
215 South Work Street, Falconer, N.Y. 14733
(716) 665-6111
www.dec.state.ny.us

One-mile long Bear Lake has clear water but a rather boring wooded shoreline, devoid of nooks and crannies. Head south, down the lake to paddle the much more interesting, narrow, winding outlet to County Road 380. Along the way you're likely to pass people fishing. This lake is full of walleye, northern pike, perch, musky, crappie and bass.

Near the DEC launch is The Clever Store complex. It consists of a snack bar, campground, antique store, marine and tackle shop, with canoe, pontoon boat and paddleboat rentals.

Paddling Directions:
- Either paddle around Bear Lake or head south to the outlet.
- County Road 380 is as far south as you can paddle.

Date visited:

Notes:

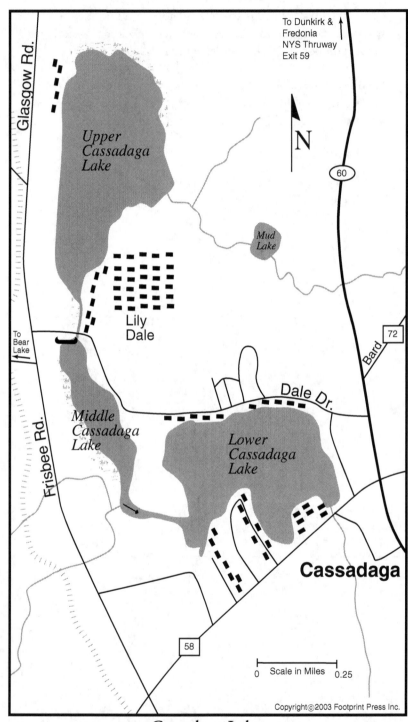

Cassadaga Lakes

34

CASSADAGA LAKES

Location: Cassadaga and Lily Dale, Chautauqua County

Directions: From the New York State Thruway (I-90) take exit 59 at Dunkirk and Fredonia. Head south on Route 60 for 8 miles. Turn right (W) on Dale Drive at a sign for Lily Dale. Pass Lower Lake, Middle Lake and the entrance to Lily Dale, then cross the bridge connecting Upper and Middle Lakes. The parking area and launch will be on the left across the bridge. It's marked by a brown DEC sign "Cassadaga Lake Fishing Access Site."

Launch Site #1: A sloped gravel ramp and dock at the 20-car parking area.

Best Season to Visit: Spring, summer and fall

Paddling Distance: Launch to the North end of Upper Lake: 0.8 mile
Launch to the SE end of Lower Lake: 1.1 mile
Paddle around Upper Cassadaga Lake: 2 miles
Paddle around Middle Cassadaga Lake: 1.4 miles
Paddle around Lower Cassadaga Lake: 2 miles

Estimated Time to Paddle: 1 to 4 hours

Difficulty: ▬▬●

Other Activities: None

Amenities: Picnic table and Porta-Potty at the launch

Dogs: OK

Admission: Free

Contact: DEC, Region 9
215 South Work Street, Falconer, N.Y. 14733
(716) 665-6111
www.dec.state.ny.us

Spirits may accompany you as you paddle these lakes. Lily Dale Assembly, a Spiritualist community now in its 123rd year, sits on the shore of Upper Cassadaga Lake. During the summer season Lily Dale welcomes visitors and offers lectures, demonstrations and services on psychic phenomena, clairvoyance and spiritual healing.

A white swan that lives on Cassadaga Lake.

The launch puts you in Middle Cassadaga Lake. This is the narrowest of the three lakes and sports a combination of cottages and undisturbed tree-lined shoreline. You can follow it south to Lower Cassadaga Lake, which is ringed with cottages but offers an interesting convoluted shoreline to explore. Or, head north, paddling under the bridge to Upper Cassadaga Lake. Lily Dale is on the southeast shore and a few cottages dot the northwest shore; otherwise this lake is undeveloped. In addition to any spirits that drift your way, you'll probably be accompanied by some large white swans. They're Lily Dale residents, but they wander the entire lake and like to greet visitors.

Paddling Directions:
 • Paddle at will.

Date visited:

Notes:

Paddles in Niagara, Erie, Orleans and Genesee Counties

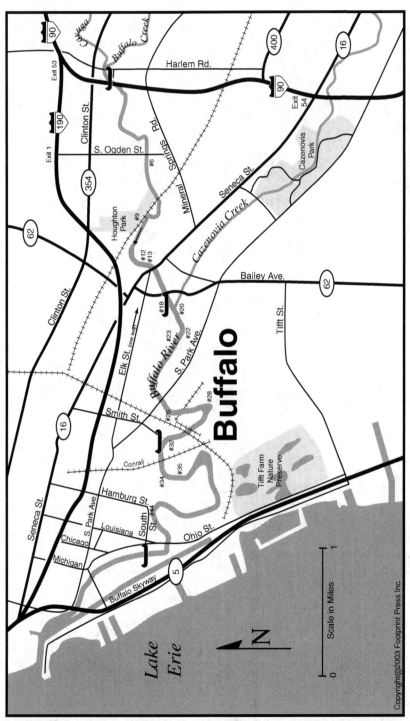

Buffalo River Urban Canoe Trail (West Seneca to Buffalo)

35

BUFFALO RIVER URBAN CANOE TRAIL
(West Seneca to Buffalo)

Location: West Seneca and Buffalo, Erie County

Directions: From I-90 take exit 53 to I-190 ($0.50 toll) toward downtown Buffalo. Take exit 1 immediately after the toll booth and follow the signs to go south on South Ogden Street. Turn left onto Clinton Street, pass under I-90 and turn right on Harlem Road. Turn right at the brown & yellow DEC sign "Buffalo River - Harlem Road Fishing Access Site" next to Tops.

Launch Site : The DEC Harlem Road Access Site has parking for 15 cars and a 25-yard path to a mud and gravel shore for hand launching.

Take-out Site #1: Enter the South Buffalo Pump Station of the Buffalo Sewer Authority on the northwest side of the Bailey Avenue bridge. Park before the closed gate. It's a long narrow trail through high scrub to a mud beach at the shore. This is a marginal access point.

Take-out Site #2: At the end of Smith Street is a park with a sloped path to water level. Park in the circle at the end of the dog-leg near the start of the paved bike path.

Take-out Site #3: DEC access site on Ohio Street just north of South Street, next to Great Lakes Paper, is marked by a brown and yellow DEC sign "Buffalo River - Ohio Street." There's parking for 15 cars and a short carry to a sloped cement hand launch.

Best Season to Visit: Spring, summer and fall

Paddling Distance: Total: 6.5 miles

        Harlem Road to Bailey Avenue: 2.0 miles
        Bailey Avenue to Smith Street: 2.0 miles
        Smith Street to Ohio Street take-out: 2.5 miles

Estimated Time to Paddle: 4 hours, one way

Difficulty: ▬■ (no discernable flow in summer)

CAUTION: If you see a lake freighter, move to the shore, away from a bend or bridge. The current from the bow or stern propellers of a lake freighter can capsize a small boat or draw it into the side of the ship. If you hear five or more whistle blasts, move to shore immediately.

Amenities: None
Dogs: OK
Admission: Free
Contact: DEC, Region 9
270 Michigan Avenue, Buffalo, NY 14203-2999
(716) 851-7010

The Buffalo River basin was once a pristine waterway, draining an extensive northern forest. Settlers moved to the area and converted the surrounding land to farms and later to industrial uses. By the 1960s the river was polluted and citizen and government groups worked together to significantly improve the water quality. It's an ongoing process. Today, the Buffalo River does not follow its pre-1800s course. It has been modified, deepened and rechanneled. In its natural state, it was only navigable by canoe.

Paddling this waterway gives you a perspective on development that can only be seen from water level. As you paddle toward Buffalo, you'll pass through three sections designated the Natural River, the Urban River and the Industrial River. My initial impression was, "this is Buffalo?" The trip begins through greenery with only a spattering of residences visible. Then the industrialized portion begins and along with it, your history lesson.

The DEC, in conjunction with other groups, have placed numbers on blue water wave signs at pilings or bulkheads to identify sites of interest along the trail. We'll use those numbers below. For a more comprehensive guide to this canoe trail, packed with local history, write to the DEC Region 9 office.

Paddling Directions:
- Head left, downstream under the big (and noisy) I-90 bridge.
- This is the most natural section, where you're likely to see animals, but it has been moved, straightened and altered for erosion control.

- Watch for site #2, the West Seneca Sewer District #6 Overflow Retention Facility, which receives and holds heavy rainwater flows, so they can be treated before release into the river.
- Site #4 to the left is a flood plain forest composed of cotton-woods, willows and other plants that tolerate flooding.
- Pass under the brown Ogden Street bridge.
- Watch for fish near site #7, where vegetation forms a canopy over the river. The shade allows the water to retain oxygen, which attracts fish. Archeologists speculate that this was the site of a 1600s Iroquois Indian village of Long Houses.
- Pass under the Conrail bridge (a rusted trestle), site #8. It was built by the Pennsylvania Railroad to connect Harrisburg, PA to Buffalo. To your right, before and after this bridge is Houghton Park (a.k.a. Stachowski Park and site #9), which sits on fill in the flood plain.
- Now you're entering the urban section with fewer animals and more homes and businesses.
- To your left is site #10, a wetland, best described as a backwater slough (pronounced slew).
- The Niagara Mohawk facility on your right (site #11) marks the site where Cazenovia Creek originally met Buffalo Creek and the site of the Seneca Council House. Major treaties were signed here between 1780 and 1842 that determined present day Iroquois land holdings in Western New York.
- The beavers are back in the Buffalo River after a century-long absence. Watch for their tree cuttings and a den built into the left bank (site #12).
- Continue watching the left bank for a colony of bank swal-lows (site #13). The burrows are 18 to 36 inches deep and lead to a nest chamber lined with straw, grass and feathers.
- Pass under the brown Seneca Street bridge. Look up to see a pipe bridge 100 feet above (site #16). Originally built in 1927, it carried five pipelines. Today it carries two pipelines for National Fuel Gas that ensure a second source of gas for South Buffalo in case the major supplies southwest of the city are disrupted.
- Pass under the old brown Bailey Avenue bridge.

A grain elevator along the Buffalo River.

- On the right bank notice the South Buffalo Pump Station (site #18), which pumps sewage to the Bird Island Wastewater Treatment Plant. Just past it is a mud landing leading away from the river. This is take-out site #1.
- Cazenovia Creek (site #20) merges from the left to join the Buffalo River for its final 5.5-mile journey to Lake Erie. (Paddle up the creek if you wish, 1.2 miles to a launch in Cazenovia Park.)
- Pass pilings for the old Delaware, Lackawanna and Western liftbridge (a.k.a. Oxbow Railroad bridge), which was built in 1913. This former liftbridge and the high pipeline bridge previously passed are evidence that planners expected this section to be industrialized and receive large boat traffic. That never happened and the bridge was only raised for testing. The bridge was recently demolished.
- You're now entering the industrialized section and the farthest inland that lake freighters travel. If you see one, move to the shore immediately.
- Pass a large greenhouse operation to the left.

- The long concrete wall to your right (site #23) marks the wharf where Mobil Oil freighters used to deliver oil. Today, this site receives 11,000 barrels of oil daily from New Jersey (mostly for use by gas stations), but they're delivered by pipeline. Notice the smell of oil permeating the air and look for bubbles percolating to the surface. Perhaps this isn't the best place to go for a swim or practice your eskimo roll. The low round white structures are above-ground storage tanks. Oil refining began here in the 1880s but ceased in the 1990s.
- The next set of tanks downstream belongs to PVS Chemicals, Inc., a manufacturer of sulfuric acid and other chemicals. The recycling of spent sulfuric acid began in this area in the 1880s. For years they discharged waste directly into the river. That changed back in the 1960s.
- Pass under the huge, brown metal South Park Avenue bridge (site #25), built in 1953. On the left, upstream, look for a ramp and green vehicles. These are icebreakers used by the City of Buffalo during winter to keep the river open.
- To the right is site #26, Buffalo Color Corporation, the largest supplier of indigo dye in the world. Chances are the dye used to color your bluejeans was made here.
- Pass another Delaware, Lackawanna and Western liftbridge, built in 1913 to carry passenger trains from New York City. Only the right half remains.
- On the left is site #28, the former Republic Steel. (Buffalo Color Corporation is still on the right.) Steel manufacturing began here in 1907 and closed in 1982. It was torn down in 1992.
- #29 is the site of a remedial action plan to clean the river and its sediments from years of pollution by the National Aniline Dye Company (Buffalo Color Corporation).
- Site #30 is the warehouse to the left with "August Feine and Sons" on the roof. Before it was demolished in the 1980s, a plant located here cooked coal in the absence of air to make coke, a fuel used in steel manufacturing.
- Pass under an active Conrail bridge, then the Norfolk Southern bridge.

- Site #32 to the left was Hobo Jungle, a shanty town for railroad hobos during the 1930s Great Depression.
- To the right is a metal and cement dock with a slope to Smith Street Park. (This is take-out site #2.)
- Pass under another active Conrail liftbridge.
- Look to the right to find site #34, Airco Industrial Gases, which separates atmospheric gas into its components to produce oxygen, nitrogen and argon.
- Concrete Central, site #35 will be on the left. Several companies joined together around 1915 to build this series of grain elevators - the largest in the world at the time. It closed in 1973.
- Further downstream on the left is site #36 the Cargill-Superior grain elevator built in 1915.
- The junkyard to the left is actually flattened cars being recycled at Co-Steel Recycling, site #37. They can scrap 500 cars a day.
- On the right is Booth Oil, a waste oil processing plant and site #38.
- On the left is the Marine A grain elevator, built around 1925, followed by the Lake & Rail elevator sporting a ConAgra logo.
- Look right to see the dock for 2 tugboats. They guide freighters through the river's winding turns.
- Perot Elevator (site #42) and American Elevator (site #43) on the left were built around 1907 and are used today for grain storage by ConAgra.
- The Pillsbury Standard Elevator on the right (site #44) is the largest elevator presently operating in Buffalo.
- Just before the next bridge is Electric Elevator, built in 1987 and replaced in 1940.
- Pass under the huge metal superstructure of the Ohio Street bridge. This vertical lift bridge was built in 1962 to replace several previous bridges dating back to the early 1800s.
- On the left are the storage elevators of the LaFarge Cement Corporation. Across the river are pleasure boats docked at the Bison City Rod & Gun Club, site #48.
- Great Lakes Paper Fibres, the black building on the right, buys and sells waste paper.

Ohio Street liftbridge over the Buffalo River.

- Bear right to the Ohio Street take-out point, a sloped ramp lined with big grey boulders. (Across the river is a large building labeled ADM Milling Co.)

Date visited:

Notes:

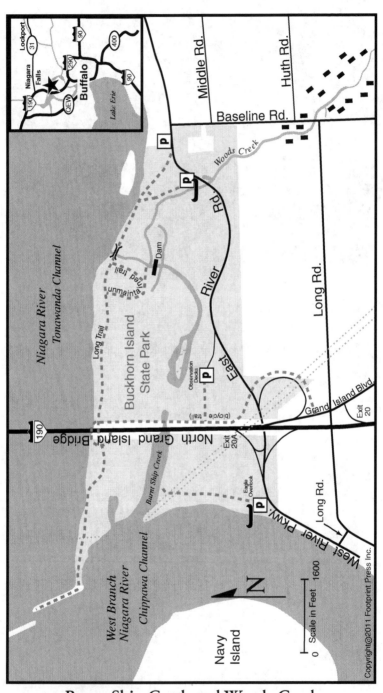

Burnt Ship Creek and Woods Creek

36

BURNT SHIP & WOODS CREEKS

Location: Buckhorn Island State Park, Grand Island, Erie County

Directions: If traveling north on I-190, take exit 20 (Long Road). Turn left (W) on Grand Island Boulevard, then right (N) on Long Road. At the end, turn left onto Baseline Road. At the end turn left onto East River Road and park at the second parking area on the right marked by a brown sign "Woods Creek Parking Area." If heading south on I-190, take exit 20A. Turn left and follow East River Road to the Woods Creek parking area.

Launch & Take-out Site: The launch next to the parking lot is steep, but wood-chip lined.

Best Season to Visit: Spring, summer and fall

Nearby Campgrounds: Niagara Falls KOA, 2570 Grand Island Boulevard, Grand Island, NY 14072 (716) 773-7583

Cinderella Campsite, 2797 Grand Island Boulevard, Grand Island, NY 14072 (716) 773-2872

Paddling Distance: 2.8 miles round trip (About 0.7-mile on Woods Creek and 0.7-mile on Burnt Ship Creek each way)

Estimated Time to Paddle: 1.5 hours to explore north of East River Road, 0.5 hour to explore Woods Creek south of East River Road

Difficulty: (easy waterway, but it does involve a short portage over a small dam)

Other Activities: Hike, bike, fish, bird watch

Amenities: None

Dogs: OK on leash (must pick up after pet)

Admission: Free, dawn to dusk (there is a toll charge when crossing the Grand Island bridge)

Contact: Buckhorn Island State Park
c/o Beaver Island State Park
2136 West Oakfield Road, Grand Island, NY 14072
(716) 773-3271

Buckhorn Island State Park sits at the northwest point of Grand Island. It's an island by virtue of narrow streams called Burnt Ship Creek and Woods Creek, which bisect this 895 acres of marsh, meadows, and woods. A 2.6-mile-long (each way) hiking trail leads along the shoreline of the Niagara River under the North Grand Island Bridge to the tip of a jetty. It affords great views of the river, other shorelines, marshes, and many flocks of resident geese, ducks, and gulls. In 2001 a paved bike path, additional parking areas, and observation platforms were added to this park.

The Niagara River corridor was officially designated an "Important Bird Area" in December, 1996. Nineteen species of gulls have been found here, representing almost half of the world's 45 species. The area is also on the migration route for 25 species of waterfowl. The most numerous gulls found here are Bonaparte's gull, ring-billed gull, and herring gull. The most common waterfowl to be found are greater scaup ducks, common mergansers, and canvasbacks. Be sure to take your binoculars.

The paddling is through a wetland of grasses and cattails on 60-foot-wide Burnt Ship Creek. There was a negligible current during low water conditions in November. Woods Creek winds through backyards until it becomes too narrow and shallow to paddle.

Wildlife is bountiful in this area. We chased a muskrat through the water and saw two beaver dams along the edge of the creeks. Great blue herons and ducks scurried out of our way. We paddled quietly past a sleeping deer along the bank of Woods Creek. If you paddle in spring, the many bird nest boxes along the channel may have residents.

Paddling Directions up Woods Creek: (0.5 hour round trip)

- From the launch area (on the north side of East River Road), head left on Woods Creek to go under the East River Road bridge.
- Pass a side channel to the left (leads to the old grassy launch area on the south side of East River Road).
- Pass under Baseline Road bridge.
- Bear left as a small creek comes in from the right.
- Soon Woods Creek becomes too shallow and you have to turn around.

Paddling Directions up Burnt Ship Creek: (1.5 hours round trip)

- From the launch area (on the north side of East River Road), head to the right on Woods Creek.
- Continue down Woods Creek to a "T." (Left is a dam and right is the Niagara River.)
- Turn right and paddle out to the Niagara River, passing under a pedestrian bridge before reaching the river. The Niagara River is a swift channel that leads to Niagara Falls, so it's not recommended for canoes and kayaks.
- Turn around at the river and paddle back up the channel.
- This time bear right and approach the dam on the right bank. A grassy area is available for the short portage.
- Just after the dam are dead-end channels to the right and left that you can explore if you wish.
- Paddle the middle channel (Burnt Ship Creek), straight from the dam.
- Turn right into the next channel and the cattail-lined waterway will widen.
- As you approach the North Grand Island Bridge it will get noisier. The channel bends left and loops back toward the dam. (There is no channel available to access the North Grand Island bridge or the Niagara River on this side.)
- Pass an observation area on your right then continue straight past a channel to the left (this was your outward bound leg).
- Bear left to portage over the dam.
- After the dam bear right up Woods Creek.
- Paddle under the East River Road bridge.
- Turn left into the side channel to the launch area.

Date visited:

Notes:

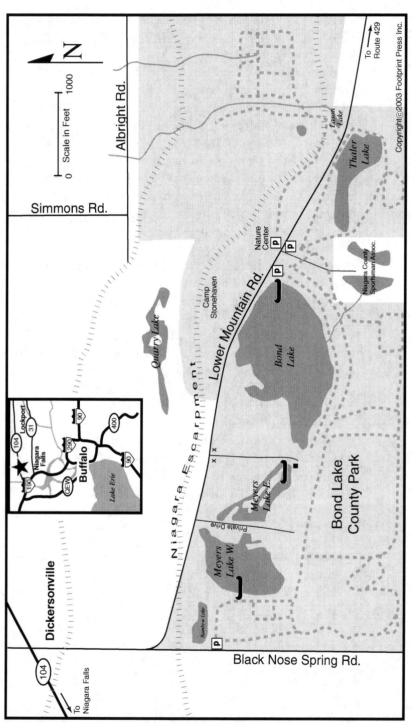

Bond Lake

37

BOND LAKE

Location: Bond Lake County Park, 2571 Lower Mountain Road, Lewiston, Niagara County

Directions: From Route 104, turn south on Route 429. Take the second right onto Lower Mountain Road. Pass the nature center, then turn left into the Bond Lake parking area.

Launch Site #1: At the Bond Lake parking area, you'll find an easy grass bank launch.

Launch Site #2: The access road to the east end of Meyers Lake East is between two willow trees marked with red Xs. Parking is at the end of the access road, near an abandoned house. The launch is a flat rock ledge that creates an easy launch site. The road between Meyers Lake East and Meyers Lake West is private, but it's a short and easy carry between the lakes.

Launch Site #3: Park at the parking area off Black Nose Spring Road and carry 900 feet along a dirt path to launch at the west end of Meyers Lake West.

Best Season to Visit: Spring, summer and fall

Nearby Campgrounds: Niagara County Camping Resort
                              7369 Wheeler Road, Lockport, NY
                              (716) 434-3991, www.niagaracamping.com

Paddling Distance: A loop around the edges of all three lakes with portages in between is 2 miles
                              Bond Lake is 0.4 mile long
                              Meyers Lake East is 0.2 mile long
                              Meyers Lake West is 0.1 mile long

Estimated Time to Paddle: 1 to 2 hours

Difficulty: ▶━◣ (to paddle any single lake)

                    ▶━◣ ▶━◣ (to portage between lakes)

Other Activities: Fish, hike

Amenities: Picnic tables, playground, Porta-potties in the park, nature center

Dogs: OK on leash, pick up after your pet

Paddle with the geese on Meyers Lake in Bond Lake County Park.

Admission: Free, open 7 AM - 9 PM
Contact: Niagara County Department of Parks and Recreation
314 Davidson Road, Lockport, NY 14094
(716) 439-7950

Bond Lake is a fun paddle on a pristine lake, but the Meyers Lakes are especially scenic, with irregular shorelines cradled by trees that shelter a paddler from winds. It's easy to portage from one lake to the next and explore these lakes that sit above the Niagara Escarpment.

Bond Lake County Park covers 545 acres and is dotted with lakes. It's encircled by 13 miles of hiking trails, which means you can explore it by land as well as by sea. The lakes are used by migrating waterfowl in spring and fall. Since June 1999, the Parks Department has been actively working to reduce weeds in these lakes. Their methods have included mechanical removal, stocking Triploid Grass Carp (a weed-eating fish), and mechanical aeration.

The nature center on Lower Mountain Road is run by volunteers and is only open Sundays from noon to 4PM. The building it's in serves mainly as a warming hut for the many winter activities in this park, such a sledding, ice skating and cross-country skiing.

Paddling Directions:
- Launch into Bond Lake from the Bond Lake County Park parking area off Lower Mountain Road.
- Paddle west across Bond Lake, hugging whichever shore you prefer.
- At the west end of the lake, portage across to Meyers Lake East.
- At the west end of the lake, portage across to Meyers Lake West.
- Reverse this process to head back to your car, only this time paddle along the opposite shorelines.

Date visited:

Notes:

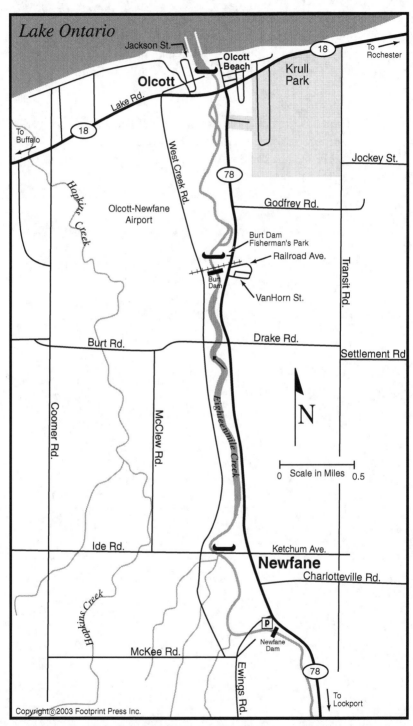

Eighteenmile Creek (Burt Dam to Olcott)

38

EIGHTEENMILE CREEK
(Burt Dam to Olcott)

Location: Newfane and Olcott, Niagara County

Directions: From Lockport head north on Route 78, past Route 104 and through Newfane. After Burt Dam, look to the left for Burt Dam Fisherman's Park.

Launch Site #1: Burt Dam Fisherman's Park has a large parking area with a 100-yard carry to a sloped, paved ramp.

Take-out Site: From Route 18 (Lake Road) along Lake Ontario in Olcott, turn north toward the lake on Jackson Street. At the stop sign, turn right onto West Main Street. At the end on the right will be Town of Newfane Marina and Park with a parking area and a short paved ramp with docks.

Best Season to Visit: May through August (September through April this area is choked with fishermen in motor boats)

Nearby Campgrounds: Harbor Resort Campground (across from the marina), 5764 Lake Road, Olcott, NY 14126 (716) 778-5190

Paddling Distance: 2 miles, one way

Estimated Time to Paddle: 0.5 to 1 hour each way

Difficulty: ▶━━●

Other Activities: Fish, bird watch

Amenities: Burt Dam Fisherman's Park has a Porta-potty
Town of Newfane Marina and Park has a shelter, picnic tables and Porta-potties

Dogs: OK

Admission: Free at Burt Dam Fisherman's Park
Town of Newfane Marina and Park, parking is free, launch or take-out of a canoe or kayak costs $3

The site of Burt Dam was first developed in 1811 when James Van Horn built a grist mill along Eighteenmile Creek. The mill didn't last long, however, as it was burned by the British during the War of 1812. The hamlet of Burt is named after Burt Van Horn, James' son.

Today, the Burt Dam Facility is a 600-kilowatt hydroelectric generating facility and dam located in the town of Burt, two miles south of Olcott. The electric power is purchased and distributed by Niagara Mohawk.

Between the Conrail railroad bridge and the dam is a prime fishing location. 500 to 800 people per day fish the mile below the dam primarily between September and April. That's why we paddlers should head here between May and August so we don't get snared by fishing lines. DEC is developing underwater diverters for the creek at the dam to enhance spawning grounds for trout and salmon. They may install fish ladders at Burt Dam.

We were awed by this waterway. We put in expecting to see a channel lined by docks and boats. Instead, we found ourselves in a pristine valley where great blue herons swooped overhead and duck-weed parted as our paddles sliced through the water. Yes, there are a few docks with boats, but they look out of place along the shores that alternate between woods and cattails. Our biggest surprise was the water itself. Crystal clear and deep, we could look down and see seaweed waving in the current below. Fish, both large and small, darted among the fronds. We felt like we were floating on the surface of an aquarium. Shortly after launching, we set our paddles down and drifted while enjoying the scene unfold below our kayaks.

You can paddle this route two ways. The route described is to put in at Burt Dam and paddle downstream to Olcott for 2 miles. If you don't want to mess with spotting a car at the end, put in at either end and make it a 4-mile round trip. When we paddled in July the current was almost nonexistent. Whatever you do, take time to play here. Watch the fish near the Burt Dam launch and poke about in the cattail marshes.

Another potential paddle route is to launch at Ide Road in Newfane and paddle 4.4 miles round tip to Burt Dam and back. On the east side of the Ide Road bridge in an unmarked dirt parking area for 10 cars and a 30-yard carry down an old dirt road to a nice launch area. You'd have to paddle this in late spring or early summer.

By late July we found the water in the creek too shallow and swift to be able to easily return upstream and the reservoir above the dam was choked in duckweed. There is no access at Burt Road or from above the dam—the water sits in a very deep valley.

We attempted to paddle farther upstream on Eighteenmile Creek from Route 104 to Newfane, but found logjams, poor access and a miserable portage at the Newfane dam, so we don't recommend it.

Paddling Directions:
- From Burt Dam Fisherman's Park, head right, downstream, away from the dam and high railroad bridge. (It used to be the Rome, Watertown and Ogdensburg Railroad.)
- Early on, plan to take time to float and enjoy the underwater scene.
- Pass a few boats at docks (but no visible buildings).
- Pass under the high cement Route18 bridge and enter *marina central*.
- Pass several docks loaded with boats then watch left for the large marina launch ramps. (You could continue out to Lake Ontario if you want.)

Date visited:

Notes:

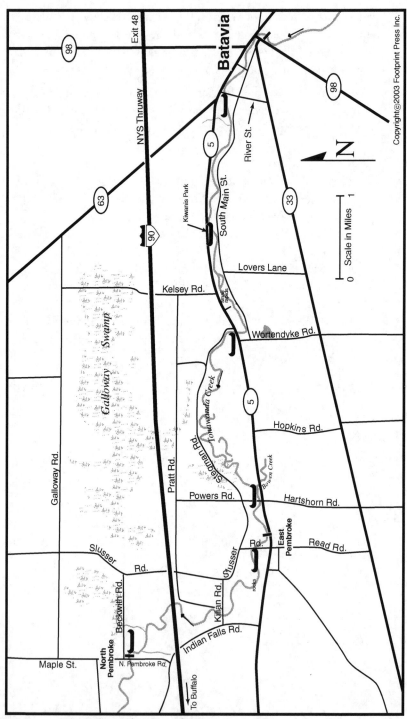

Tonawanda Creek (Batavia to North Pembroke)

39

TONAWANDA CREEK
(Batavia to North Pembroke)

Location: Batavia and Pembroke, Genesee County

Directions: From I-90 take exit 48, Batavia. Head south on Route 98 into Batavia then west on Route 5. In 0.6 mile, turn south onto River Street and look for First Niagara Bank.

Launch Site #1: Park in the back corner of the First Niagara Bank parking lot. Launch downstream, right of the River Street bridge.

Launch Site #2: Kiwanis Park off Route 5 has a steep mud bank.

Launch Site #3: Park west of the Route 5 bridge. A grass slope provides water access downstream, left.

Launch Site #4: Park along the road at the Powers Road bridge. A grass slope provides water access upstream, left.

Launch Site #5: A dirt ramp provides vehicle access to below the Slusser Road bridge. There's a nice gravel landing under the bridge, left.

Take-out Site: The North Pembroke Road bridge in North Pembroke, between the old dam and the bridge, left. Park along the road south of the bridge.

Best Season to Visit: Spring (may require pushing through shallow sections other times)

Paddling Distance: 12 miles

        River Street to Route 5: 3.5 miles

        Route 5 to Slusser Road: 4.5 miles

        Slusser Road to N. Pembroke Rd.: 3.5 miles

Estimated Time to Paddle: 3 hours in spring

Difficulty: (3.8 feet/mile gradient; one dam to portage around; one very small rapid; at the take-out you paddle through a broken down old dam)

Water Level Information: http://waterdata.usgs.gov/ny/nwis/rt (the gage, #04217000, is in Batavia, the start of this segment)

Other Activities: Fish

Amenities: Town of Batavia Kiwanis Park has picnic facilities and a playground.

Portaging around the dam on Tonawanda Creek.

Dogs: OK
Admission: Free

Mostly deep and wide with a mild current, Tonawanda Creek below Batavia is interspersed with short shallow, rocky sections that produce minor ripples. Rimmed by high mud banks, it alternates between wild sections and residential areas with some road noise.

Note: You may look on a map and think the upstream section of Tonawanda Creek between the dams in Attica and Batavia might be nice to paddle. Let us save you some agony. Sue paddled the 5 miles from Attica to Alexander in one hour with only two portages around downed trees. Rich hopped in his kayak at Alexander and attempted to head north. Five hours later, just as Sue was about to call 911 for search and rescue, he emerged from the woods, covered in mud from head to toe. He had finally left the kayak at a logjam and walked out. In this section Tonawanda Creek sits below high mud walls. It twists and turns sharply and catches every wayward tree. In 5 miles, Rich portaged 20 times over logjams. He was utterly exhausted.

Paddling Directions:

- Head downstream from River Street.
- Pass Kiwanis Park on your right. The only indication is a black plastic drain pipe sticking out from the mud bank.
- After about 3 miles, you'll pass through a narrow chute with small rapids.
- Pass under the green, metal superstructure of Route 5 bridge. (There's good off-shoulder parking and water access downstream, left.)
- Stegman Road will come close to the creek on your right repeatedly.
- Bowen Creek merges from the left.
- Shortly, pass under the low, cement, silver-railed Powers Road bridge. (Park along the road and launch upstream, right.)
- Watch for the dam ahead. It is breached on the left, but still entails a 5-foot drop. Pull-out and portage (60 yards) at the grassy area on the right bank before the dam.
- Pass under the one-lane, brown metal Slusser Road bridge. (Parking and easy access are upstream, left.)
- Pass a low rock dam. In spring you can paddle over it. In lower water it may be a minor impediment.
- Pass under the Kilian Road bridge.
- Pass under the wide highway bridge of the NYS Thruway (I-90).
- You'll see a rusted highway bridge with silver rails (North Pembroke Road) with an old, partially broken dam just before it. Paddle through the broken dam on the far right. Immediately turn left and take out on the left, before the bridge.

    Note: DO NOT continue downstream. You'll have a rough run over 20-foot high Indian Falls.

Date visited:

Notes:

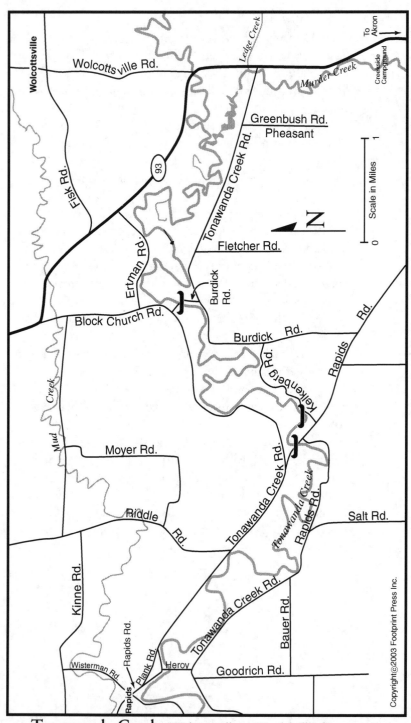

Tonawanda Creek (Wolcottsville to Wendelville) first segment

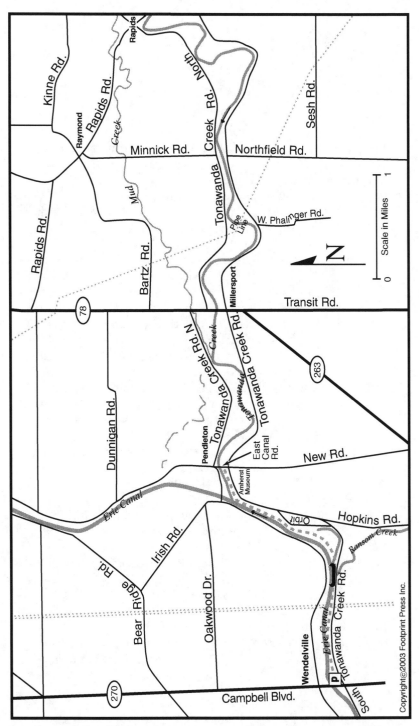

Tonawanda Creek (Wolcottsville to Wendelville) final segment

40

TONAWANDA CREEK
(Wolcottsville to Wendelville)

Location: Wolcottsville, Rapids, Pendleton and Wendelville, in Niagara & Erie Counties

Directions: Head north from Akron on Route 93. Cross Murder Creek, then turn left (W) onto Tonawanda Creek Road. Turn right onto Burdick Road. Park south of the light blue bridge along this quiet road.

Launch Site #1: From Burdick Road carry 35 yards across mowed grass to launch under the bridge at a gradual mud bank.

Launch Site #2: Off Kelkenberg Road (at the first curve from the Rapids Road corner) there's a small mowed area behind a guardrail that provides parking for 1 car. A 10-yard carry down a trail leads to a gradual mud bank with flat rocks.

Launch Site #3: Park along Rapids Road near the bridge. A 25-yard carry through tall grass leads to access down stream, right. Launch here to avoid most of the logjams.

Take-out Site: The small roadside park and picnic area off South Tonawanda Creek Road at Ransom Creek offers an easy, grassy take-out point.

Best Season to Visit: Summer

Nearby Campgrounds: Creekside Campground, 8078 Maple Road, Akron, NY 14001, (716) 542-9595

Paddling Distance: 21.2 miles

Burdick Road to Rapids Road: 5.1 miles (1.5 hrs.)
Rapids Road to Route 78: 12.1 miles
Route 78 to New Road: 2.1 miles
New Road to Ransom Creek Park: 1.9 miles

Estimated Time to Paddle: 6 to 7 hours in July

Difficulty: (some logjams, minor riffles, <one foot-per-mile average gradient)

Water Level Information: http://waterdata.usgs.gov/ny/nwis/rt
(the gage, #04218000, is in Rapids, the middle of this segment)
Other Activities: Fish
Amenities: The take-out park at Ransom Creek has picnic tables and grills
Dogs: OK
Admission: Free

This section of Tonawanda Creek wanders (literally!) through flat land, offering a peaceful ride through rural farms, fields, and woods. It only reaches developed areas for the last section from Route 78 to the takeout at Ransom Creek in Wendelville. However, it is misnamed. It should be called Mud Creek because muddy water flows between high mud banks. What you encounter will depend on the ravages of the previous spring runoffs and the water level when you paddle. In mid-July we found a gently flowing current, verdant green banks and several logjams and downed trees through which we pushed. The times we needed to portage were minimal. We encountered a few shallow spots (such as just downstream of the village of Rapids) and a few ripples. Keep an eye out for the many turtles and other wildlife, such as beavers, groundhogs, raccoons and deer that call this creekbed home. Because of the mild current in summer, it is possible to paddle upstream and do a round-trip excursion.

Note: Paddling upstream of Route 93 (from North Pembroke to Route 93) is not recommended. A significant waterfall (Indian Falls) impedes the way. High, muddy banks makes access difficult and many bridges in the Tonawanda Indian Reservation through which this section flows, are barricaded.

Paddling Directions:
- Head downstream from the blue Burdick Road bridge.
- Be wary of logjams through this winding section. Some may require tricky maneuvering to haul out and carry around or over.
- A small creek merges from the left through an 8-foot round metal culvert where Kelkenberg Road parallels the creek. (This is launch site #2.)

- At 5.1 miles, pass under the brown Rapids Road highway bridge. (Road access is downstream, right through high weeds.)
- Pass under the brown Tonawanda Creek Road highway bridge (the village of Rapids) and gaging station. (Parking is very limited nearby, but you could access the road via the riprap stones beside the bridge abutments.)
- Begin to sporadically see houses along the shore.
- The creek becomes currentless, wide, deep and river-like. In July we passed alcoves of yellow lilies.
- Pass the buried pipeline, marked by orange and white posts on the right shore.
- At 17.2 miles, pass under the brown Route 78 (Transit Road) bridge. (Park southeast of the bridge at a gravel area next to Belknap Heating & Cooling. Upstream, left is an easy stone slope.)
- Watch for Mud Creek to merge from the right.
- At 19.3 miles, pass under the brown New Road / East Canal Road bridge.
- Reach the Erie Canal and paddle left, upstream.
- Pass a second buried pipeline.
- Ransom Creek merges from the left, crossed by a rust-colored, arched pedestrian bridge. Take-out left at the grassy bank downstream from Ransom Creek. This is a small park off South Tonawanda Creek Road.

    Note: If you miss this park, you'll pass under the Route 270 bridge (it's labeled Campbell Boulevard). There is no parking or river access from this bridge, but downstream left is the Amherst Marine Center dock. Or, just before the bridge on the left is the North Amherst Fire Company. Take-out here is marginal, but it does have parking, a playground and a Porta-potty.

Date visited:

Notes:

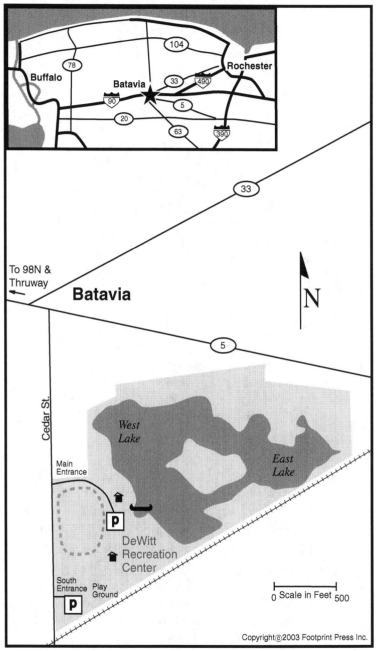

DeWitt Quarry

41

DEWITT QUARRY

Location: Batavia, Orleans County
Directions: From Route 5 at the eastern edge of Batavia, head south on Cedar Street. The entrance to DeWitt Recreation Center will be on the left.
Launch & Take-out Site: A sloped dirt ramp is on the edge of the quarry pond a short distance from the parking area in DeWitt Recreation Center.
Best Season to Visit: Spring, summer and fall
Nearby Campgrounds: Lei-Ti Campground, 9979 Francis Road, Batavia, NY 14020, 1-800-HILEITI
Paddling Distance: Approximately 1 mile around the pond
Estimated Time to Paddle: 0.5 to 1 hour
Difficulty:
Other Activities: Playground, picnic, fishing, paved loop for inline skating (swimming is not allowed)
Amenities: Restrooms
Dogs: Pets NOT allowed
Admission: Free, 9 AM - 9 PM
Contact: Genesee County Parks
153 Cedar Street, Batavia, NY 14020
(585) 344-1122

DeWitt Recreational Facility covers 63 acres of land and includes a 38-acre pond. Prior to 1935, it was used as a sand and gravel quarry by Genesee LeRoy Stone Company, a subsidiary of B. R. DeWitt, Inc. In 1993 the company donated the land to Genesee County for use as a park. This is a work in progress. Plans call for additional picnic pavilions, play areas, trails and plantings.

This is not the most scenic place to paddle. The banks of the ponds and island are gravel with small, scrub trees. However, it is a preserved example of an old quarry and offers an up-close educational experience for inquisitive families. The water has the teal blue color often seen in quarries.

Date visited:

Notes:

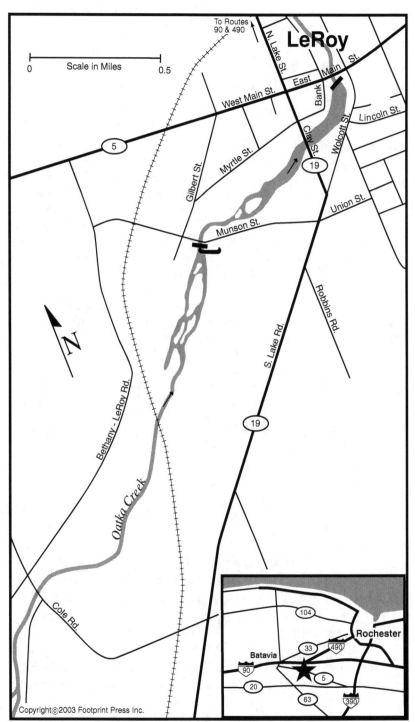

Oatka Creek (Backwaters of the LeRoy Dams)

42

OATKA CREEK
(Backwaters of the LeRoy Dams)

Location: LeRoy, Genesee County

Directions: From I-90 take exit 47 then exit 1 to head south on Route 19. In LeRoy, pass Route 5, cross over Oatka Creek then turn right (W) onto Munson Street. Park in the 10-car parking area on the left immediately before the Oatka Creek bridge. Do not block the red hydrant.

Launch & Take-out Site: The Munson Street parking area offers a wooden walkway to a fishing dock. To launch upstream from the dam cross the grass in front of the red firemen's dry-hydrant and down the gravel bank to water level. To launch downstream of the dam, follow the paved trail parallel to the road to launch from below the Munson Street bridge.

Best Season to Visit: Spring, summer and fall

Paddling Distance: 1.8 miles, round trip downstream, between dams 1.4 miles, round trip upstream, between the dam and the railroad tracks

Estimated Time to Paddle: 0.75 to 1 hour round trip, downstream 0.5 to 1 hour round trip, upstream

Difficulty: ▶━━

Other Activities: Fish, bird watch

Amenities: None

Dogs: OK

Admission: Free

Two dams hold back the waters of Oatka Creek in LeRoy, forming backwaters that are deep enough to paddle year-round (except when frozen). It's like paddling on a pond. From the central launch point at Munson Road, you can paddle upstream, above the dam, or paddle downstream, below the dam. Heading downstream, you'll find a second dam just before Route 5 (Main Street, LeRoy). Both directions offer islands around which to paddle. Downstream is more residential, but both directions are fun for a short, easy paddle. Upstream you can easily reach the railroad bridge before encountering fast, shallow water. How far you paddle upstream, past the railroad bridge will bedetermined by the water level and your propensity for paddling against a current.

The rest of Oatka Creek is managed for fishing, not padding. It's blocked by many downed trees and gets shallow quickly after spring run-off. You can launch into the Genesee River at Canawaugus Park in Scottsville and paddle upstream on Oatka Creek for a short distance.

Oatka Creek above the LeRoy Dam.

Paddling Directions - upstream:
- From the Munson Road launch above the dam, head left, away from Munson Road.
- Explore the islands and cattail marshes.
- In 0.7 mile you'll reach the single-lane, rusted railroad bridge high overhead. Fast and/or shallow water may start shortly after this bridge.
- Paddle as far as you want, then return to the launch point.

Paddling Directions - downstream:

- Launch from below the Munson Road bridge and head downstream.
- Explore the islands.
- Pass under the arched cement bridge of Route 19.
- In 0.9 mile you'll reach the wide water before the dam. Stay well away from the dam.
- Return to the launch point.

Date visited:

Notes:

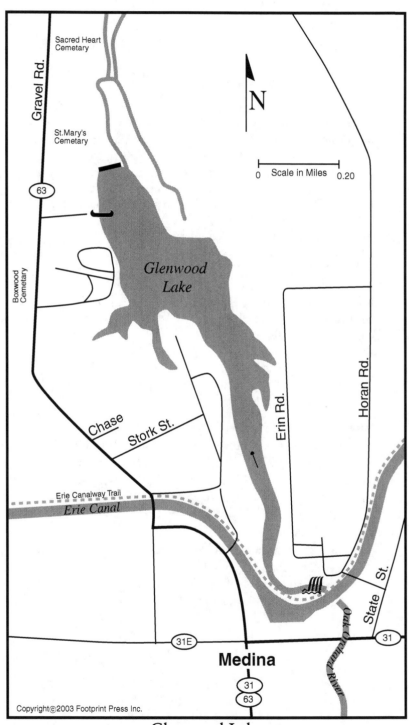

Glenwood Lake

43

GLENWOOD LAKE

Location: Medina, Orleans County

Directions: From Medina, head north on Route 63, crossing the Erie Canal. Pass Stork Street and Boxwood Cemetery, then look for the access road on the right, leading to a parking area at water's edge.

Launch & Take-out Site: A paved ramp and small metal dock off Route 63.

Best Season to Visit: Spring, summer and fall

Paddling Distance: Glenwood Lake is 1.5 miles long

Estimated Time to Paddle: 1 to 3 hours

Difficulty: ▬▬▬

Other Activities: Fishing, can walk out on the dam

Amenities: Picnic tables

Dogs: OK

Admission: Free

Contact: Glenwood Lake Boat Launch
Town of Ridgeway
1-800-724-0314

This placid lake was formed by damming Oak Orchard River. The river flows north, passing under the Erie Canal then tumbles down a waterfall (Medina Falls) before slowing its course in Glenwood Lake. Paddle south from the launch site to see Medina Falls. The dam is at the northern end, near the launch.

Paddling Directions:
- Head south from the launch to explore the bays created when the dam flooded this valley.
- At the southern end (1.5 miles from the launch), paddle up the channel to see Medina Falls.

Date visited:

Notes:

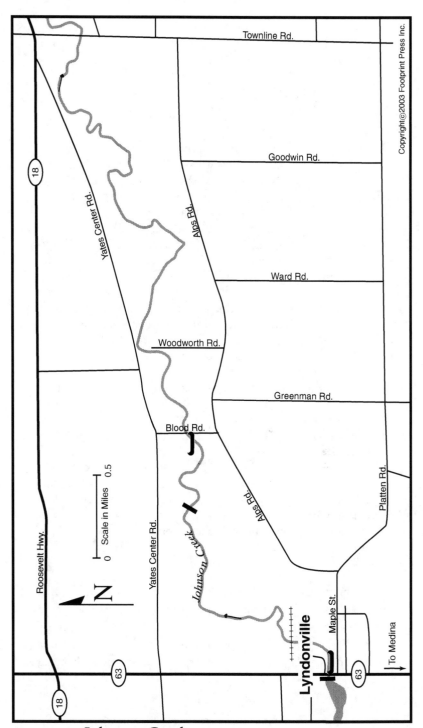

Johnson Creek (Lyndonville to Blood Road)

44

JOHNSON CREEK
(Lyndonville to Blood Road)

Location: Lyndonville, Orleans County

Directions: Take the Lake Ontario State Parkway west to its end at Lakeside Beach State Park. Continue west on Route 18. Turn south on Route 63 to Lyndonville. Or, head north from Medina on Route 63 to Lyndonville. In town, park behind the Citgo station, downstream from the Route 63 bridge and dam.

Launch Site: From the parking area behind Citgo, there's a short bank for easy access.

Take-out Site: On Blood Road there's a 1-car pull-off on the southeast side of the bridge. Across the road follow the mowed grass to shore. You'll be upstream, right of the bridge at a short grass bank.

Best Season to Visit: Spring

Nearby Campgrounds: Lakeside Beach State Park, Waterport, NY 14571, (585) 682-4888

Paddling Distance: 2.7 miles

Estimated Time to Paddle: 1 hour in mid-July

Difficulty: (moving water, a portage over a cement tractor path, in mid-July we had to push through some shallow sections)

Other Activities: Fish

Amenities: Lyndonville has a grocery store

Dogs: OK

Admission: Free

This pretty, shale-lined stream looses water by summer. We paddled in mid-July and had to drag through some shallows. It would be much easier with a bit of spring water volume. You could continue below Blood Road if the water is high enough. Still, locals told us that even in spring, you'll encounter shallows and possibly logjams.

Paddling Directions:

- Head right, downstream.
- When a railroad trestle is in view, expect a breached dam with a 2-foot drop. It's a clear run through the center.
- Pass under the large old railroad trestle.
- Portage over the 1-lane cement pad (tractor path) that spans the creek between farm fields. It's a short, easy portage.
- When you see the Blood Road bridge, watch for a grass lawn well before the bridge on the right. This is your take-out point.

Date visited:

Notes:

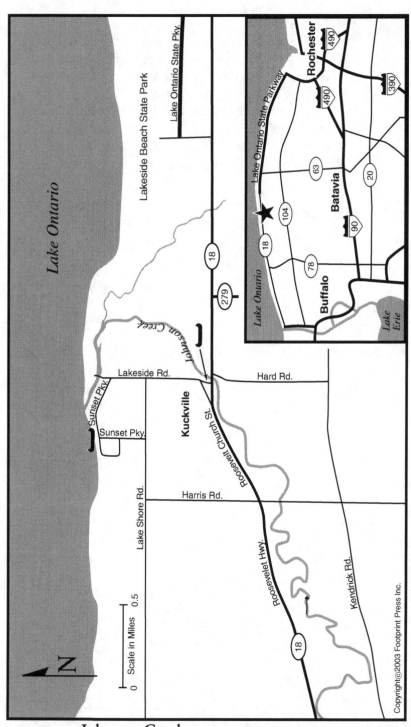

Johnson Creek (Route 18 to Lake Ontario)

45

JOHNSON CREEK

(Route 18 to Lake Ontario)

Location: Kuckville, Orleans County

Directions: Take the Lake Ontario State Parkway west to its end at Lakeside Beach State Park. Continue west on Route 18. Cross the bridge over Johnson Creek and turn right (N) onto Lakeside Road. Park at the gravel pull-off on the right across from the church.

Launch Site: From the Lakeside Road pull-off there's a short slope to the water where you launch underneath a large willow tree, among cattails.

Take-out Site: Sunset Beach Park is a small community park at the end of Sunset Parkway on Lake Ontario. Park off the road along the split-rail fence. Across the grass, 17 wooden steps lead down to a flat gravel beach.

Best Season to Visit: Summer and fall

Nearby Campgrounds: Lakeside Beach State Park, Waterport, NY 14571, (585) 682-4888

Paddling Distance: 1.7 miles from Lakeside Road to Sunset Beach Park

3.2 miles round trip in Johnson Creek

Estimated Time to Paddle: 45 minutes from Lakeside Road to Sunset Beach Park

1 hour round trip in Johnson Creek

Difficulty:  (minimal current in the creek, conditions on Lake Ontario vary tremendously)

Other Activities: Fish

Amenities: Creekside Grocery & Deli is at the northeast corner of the Route 18 bridge over Johnson Creek.

Sunset Beach Park has picnic tables.

Dogs: OK

Admission: Free

On July 6, 1759, Sir William Johnson, leading New York provincial troops, camped at the mouth of this creek en route to Fort Niagara during the French and Indian Wars. It has been called Johnson Creek ever since.

By Route 18, the creek that was shallow and winding has become deep, wide and unimpeded, making it an easy, river-like paddle. The early stretches are all greenery. The closer you get to Lake Ontario the more cottages you'll see.

Paddling Directions:
- Head left, downstream from the Lakeside Road launch point. (Or, head upstream until you reach an impediment, then return downstream.)
- Pass under the sloped, silver metal Lakeside Road bridge.
- At the mouth of the creek determine (based on lake conditions) if you want to return upstream or turn left into Lake Ontario. Expect a strong cross current near the mouth of the creek.
- Sunset Beach Park's beach is hard to spot from the water. Look for wooden steps between a beige house and an American flag.

Date visited:

Notes:

Definitions

Abutments: Pillars of stone and/or cement that support or used to support a bridge.

Aqueduct: A stone, wood, or cement trough built to carry canal water over an existing creek or river. The world's largest aqueduct for its time was built in Rochester to span the Genesee River. Eleven stone arches were erected, spanning 804 feet, to withstand the annual floods of this wild river.

Bog: An acid-rich, wet, poorly drained, spongy area characterized by plants such as sedges, heaths, and sphagnum.

CCC: Civilian Conservation Corps - a depression era work force that built public works projects across the USA. Many of the facilities in our parks (shelters, walk ways, etc.) resulted from CCC projects.

Chutes: A place where water gets squeezed to run quickly through a narrow passage.

Class I water: Waterways are categorized into classes from I to VI based on level of paddling difficulty. Class I is clear, wide channels with small waves, obstructions or hazards.

Culvert: A round metal or stone tube allowing water to pass under a road or embankment.

Dam: A barrier constructed across a waterway to control the flow or raise the level of water.

DEC: Department of Environmental Conservation

Dike: An earthen bank constructed to hold water.

DPW: Department of Public Works

Drumlin: An elongated or oval hill created from glacial debris.

Dry hydrant: A spigot that allows fire fighters to attach hoses and quickly pump water from a stream for fire fighting.

Embankment: A man-made, high dirt wall built to contain a canal such as the Great Embankment built for the Erie Canal to cross the Irondequoit Creek valley.

Esker: A long ridge formed when rivers flowed under a glacier in an ice tunnel. Rocky material accumulated on the tunnel beds, and when the glacier melted, a ridge of rubble remained.

Feeder: A diverted stream, brook, or other water source used to maintain water level in the canal.

Gabion: A wire mesh basket filled with earth and stones, used in constructing dams and reinforcing shorelines.

Guard gate: A metal gate that can be lowered to stop water flow in a canal.

Kame: A hill formed by rivers that flowed on top of a glacier and spilled over the edge depositing soil into huge piles.

Kettle hole: A depression pond created when a large block of ice separated from a glacier. Water running off of the glacier deposited gravel and debris all around the ice block. The block melted, leaving behind a rough circular depression.

Logjam: Trees and branches that fall into the stream, accumulate at sharp bends and create a dam.

Neoprene: A synthetic rubber used in weather-resistant products.

Oxbow: Rivers and streams that wind through soft soils create oxbows, or u-shaped loops.

Pool: A deep or still place in a stream.

Portage: To carry or drag your boat over or around an impediment.

Marsh: An area of soft, wet land.

Meander: To follow a winding or twisting course. It derives from the Meander River in western Turkey that is notable for its twists and turns.

PFD: A personal floatation device or life preserver worn to keep you afloat in case of a tip over.

Riffle: An area of fast-moving, shallow water.

Rookery: The nesting and breeding ground of certain birds such as great blue herons.

Slough: Also spelled slue. Pronounced slew. A stagnant swamp, marsh, bog, or pond, especially as part of an inlet or backwater.

Strainer:	A tree across the waterway where the main current of water passes through the tree. In effect, the water passes through the tree, but you get hung up in the branches, strained out. Due to the pressure of moving water, you can be trapped underwater in a strainer and drown. Strainers are also prone to bending boats in half.
Swamp:	Wet, spongy land saturated and sometimes partially or intermittently covered with water. Or, to tip your boat over and have it fill with water.
Topo map:	Short for topographic map. It's a map showing elevation changes using gradient lines.
USGS:	United States Geological Survey, the branch of government that produces topographic maps.
Waste weir:	A dam along the edge of a canal that allows overflow water to dissipate to a side waterway. A type of spillway.
Weir:	A dam placed across a river or canal to raise or divert the water, as for a millrace, or to regulate or measure the flow.
White water:	Turbulent water that creates frothy white caps.
WPA:	Works Progress Administration

Canoe & Kayak Rentals

Rentals in Monroe, Livingston and Steuben Counties:

BayCreek Paddling Center
1099 Empire Blvd., Rochester, NY 14609
(585) 288-2830, www.baycreek.com

Bayside Boat & Tackle
40 Mariners Drive, Rochester, NY 14617
(585) 224-8289, www.baysideboatandtackle.com

Canadice Lake Outfitters
6773 Canadice Lake Rd, Springwater, NY 14560
(585) 669-9512, canadicelakeoutfitters@gmail.com

Cooperstown Rentals
6000 St. Route 80, Cooperstown NY 13326
607.286.7349, https://www.canoeandkayakrentals.com/

Erie Canal Boat Company
7 Liftbridge Lane West, Fairport, NY 14450
(585) 748-2628, www.eriecanalboatcompany.com/

Genesee Waterways Center
(rentals available Friday, Saturday, Sunday)
149 Elmwood Ave., Rochester, NY 14611
(585) 328-3960, www.geneseewaterways.org

Keuka Watersports
8533 State Route 54, Hammondsport, NY 14840
607-569-2889

Lighthouse Kayak and Canoe Rental
22 E Buffalo St, Churchville, New York, NY 14428
(585) 489-9867

North Country Kayak & Canoe
16878 West Lake Road, Branchport, NY 14418
(607) 868-7456, amsailing02@yahoo.com

Oak Orchard Canoe & Kayak Experts
1350 Empire Blvd., Rochester, NY 14609
(585) 288-5550, www.oakorchardcanoe.com

Portlandville PaddleSports Store & Rentals
2828 NYS Route 28, Portlandville, NY 13834
607.286.7349, https://www.canoeandkayakrentals.com/

Yankee Canoe Company
7464 County Road 77, Prattsburgh, NY 14873
(607) 522-6400

Rentals in Chautauqua, Cattaraugus and Allegany Counties:

A-1 Rent
436 S. Union Road, Olean, NY 14760
(716) 373-7368, www.a-1rentall.com

Adventure Calls Outfitters
1 (888) 270-2410
aco.rafting@gmail.com, http://www.adventure-calls.com/

Chautauqua Marina
104 West Lake Road, Mayville, NY 14757
http://www.chautauquamarina.com/index.php
(716) 753 3913

Evergreen Outfitters
4845 Route 474, Ashville, NY 14710
(716) 763-2266, www.evergreen-outfitters.com

SUP Erie Adventures
1028 S Shore Drive, Irving, New York 14081
716 868 2975, http://www.superieadventure.com/home.html

Zoar Valley Canoe & Rafting Co.
17 S. Water Street, Gowanda, NY 14070
(716) 532-2221, www.zoarvalleyrafting.com

Rentals in Niagara, Erie, Orleans, Genesee and Wyoming Counties:

Buffalo Harbor Kayak
Canalside
1 Naval Park Cove, Buffalo, New York 14202
(716) 288-5309, info@bfloharborkayak.com

Elevator Alley Kayak
65 Vandalia St., Buffalo, NY 14204
(716) 997-7925, info@elevatoralleykayak.com

Oak Orchard Canoe & Kayak Experts
2133 Eagle-Harbor-Waterport Road, Waterport, NY 14571
(800) 452-9257, www.oakorchardcanoe.com

Paths, Peaks and Paddles Inc.
1000 Ellicott Creek Road, Tonawanda, NY 14094
(716) 213-0350, www.pathspeakspaddles.com

Waterbike Adventures
11 Young St., Tonawanda, NY 14150
(716) 316 3905, http://waterbikeadventures.com/

Zoar Valley Canoe & Rafting Company
PO Box 695, Dunkirk, NY 14048
(800) 724-0696, www.zoarvalleyrafting.com

Guided Paddling Tours

BayCreek Paddling Center
1099 Empire Blvd., Rochester, NY 14609
(585)288-2830, www.baycreek.com

Belfast Canoe Rental
PO Box 186, Belfast, NY 14711
(716) 365-8129

Braddock Bay Paddlesports
416 Manitou Road, Hilton, NY 14468
(585) 392-2628, www.paddlingny.com

Erie Canal Boat Company
7 Liftbridge Lane West, Fairport, NY 14450
(585) 748-2628, www.eriecanalboatcompany.com/

Evergreen Outfitters
4845 Route 474, Ashville, NY 14710
(716) 763-2266, www.evergreen-outfitters.com

Pack, Paddle, Ski, Corp.
PO Box 82, South Lima, NY 14558-0082
(585) 346-5597, info@PackPaddleSki.com, www.PackPaddleSki.com
Local and world-wide lessons and tours.

Paths, Peaks and Paddles Inc.
1000 Ellicott Creek Road, Tonawanda, NY 14094
(716) 213-0350, www.pathspeakspaddles.com

Shuttles and/or Liveries

Bay Creek Paddling Center (on Irondequoit Creek)
1099 Empire Blvd., Rochester, NY 14609
(585)288-2830, www.baycreek.com

Oak Orchard Canoe & Kayak Experts (on Irondequoit Creek)
1350 Empire Blvd., Rochester, NY 14609
(585) 288-5550, www.oakorchardcanoe.com

Paths Peaks and Paddles Inc.
1000 Ellicott Creek Road, Tonawanda, NY 14094
(716) 213-0350, www.pathspeakspaddles.com

Triple Creek Outfitters (on the Canisteo, Cohocton and Tioga
Rivers) 1654 River Road, Lindley, NY 14858
(607) 523-8905

Canoe/Kayak Storage Systems

Talic Sport Hammocks
316 North Goodman Street, Rochester, NY 14607
(800) 843-3307, www.talic.com

Paddling Clubs:

Rochester area:

FLOW (Finger Lakes Ontario Watershed Paddler's Club)
(585) 442-6138, www.flowpaddlers.org

Adirondack Mountain Club - Genesee Valley Chapter
(585) 987-1717, www.gvc-adk.org/

Western area:

Zoar Valley Paddler's Club
9457 Harvey Road, Cattaraugus, NY 14719
(716) 257-9750
www.zoarvalleypaddlingclub.org

Adirondack Mountain Club - Niagara Frontier Chapter
http://adk-nfc.org/

General:

New York Marathon Canoe Racing
PO Box 245, Gilbertsville, NY 13776
www.nymcra.org

Fitness & Performance Paddling on the Erie Canal
http://fitnessperformancepaddling.org/#

Paddling Instruction:

Braddock Bay Paddlesports
416 Manitou Road, Hilton, NY 14468
(585) 392-2628 www.paddlingny.com

Evergreen Outfitters
4845 Route 474, Ashville, NY 14710
(716) 763-2266 www.evergreen-outfitters.com

Genesee Waterways Center
149 Elmwood Ave., Rochester, NY 14611
(585) 328-3960 www.geneseewaterways.org

Pack, Paddle, Ski, Corp.
PO Box 82, South Lima, NY 14558-0082
(585) 346-5597 www.PackPaddleSki.com

Sea Kayak Rochester
606 Madison Street, East Rochester, NY 14445
(585) 381-2104 www.seakayakrochester.com

Seayaker Outfitters
4300 Canandaigua Road, Walworth, NY 14568
(315) 524-9295 www.seayaker.com

Flow Gauges:

National Weather Service Northeast River Forecast Center
www.weather.gov/nerfc/

- Genesee River
- Black Creek
- Tonawanda Creek
- Cayuga Creek
- Cazenovia Creek
- Allegheny River
- Conewango Creek
- Oatka Creek
- Honeoye Creek
- Ellicott Creek
- Buffalo River
- Cattaraugus Creek
- Chadakoin River

(716) 532-5454
    -Cattaraugus River

(716) 468-2303
    -Genesee River in Letchworth State Park

U.S. Geology Survey - Real Time Data for New York
http://waterdata.usgs.gov/ny/nwis/rt

Waterways by Level of Difficulty

1 Paddle:

2 Paddles:

3 Paddles:

4 Paddles:

Waterways by Length

1 to 2 Mile Paddles

3 to 5 Mile Paddles

3 to 5 Mile Paddles

6 to 10 Mile Paddles

Over 10 Mile Paddles

Waterways by Season

Paddle Spring, Summer or Fall

Paddle Spring, Summer or Fall

Paddle Spring

Paddle Summer

Paddle Summer

Paddle Spring and Summer

Paddle Summer and Fall

Paddle Spring and Fall

On-site Camping Available

Round Trip Paddling Possible

Word Index

Word Index

Word Index

Word Index

About the Authors

The authors, Rich and Sue Freeman, decided to make their living from what they love—being outdoors. In 1996 they left corporate jobs to spend six months hiking 2,200 miles on the Appalachian Trail from Georgia to Maine. That adventure deepened their love of the outdoors and inspired them to share this love by introducing others to the joys of hiking.

Since most people don't have the option (let alone the desire) to undertake a six-month trek, they decided to focus on short hikes near home. The result was the first edition of *Take A Hike! Family Walks in the Rochester Area*. They went on to explore hiking, bicycling, skiing, and snowshoeing trails, waterfalls and now waterways for paddling throughout central and western New York State. This is their 10th guidebook.

Rich and Sue are active members of several area outdoors groups. In addition, their passion for adventure continues. They have hiked the 500-mile-long Bruce Trail in Ontario, Canada, hiked on the Florida Trail, hiked across northern Spain on the Camino de Santiago Trail and hiked a 500-mile section of the International Appalachian Trail in Quebec, Canada. They have trekked to the top of Mt. Kilimanjaro, the highest mountain in Africa. Recently (in addition to kayaking hundreds of miles of New York's waterways), they hiked the tropical forests and volcanic peaks of wild Hawaii.

On bicycles they have crossed New York State on the Erie Canalway Trail and pedaled the C&O Canal Trail from Washington D.C. to Cumberland, Maryland.

Since beginning their new careers writing and publishing guidebooks, the Freemans have pared down their living expenses and are enjoying a simpler lifestyle. They now have control of their own destiny and the freedom to head into the woods and waterways for a refreshing respite when the urge strikes. Still, their life is infinitely more cluttered than when they carried all their worldly needs on their backs for six months on the Appalachian Trail.